THE LEGENDS OF
BRADFORD CITY

THE LEGENDS OF
BRADFORD CITY

by David Markham

First published in Great Britain in 2007 by
The Breedon Books Publishing Company Limited
Breedon House, 3 The Parker Centre,
Derby, DE21 4SZ.

This paperback edition published in Great Britain in 2014 by DB Publishing, an imprint of JMD Media Ltd

© DAVID MARKHAM, 2007

All Rights Reserved. No part of this publication may be reproduced, stored in a retrieval system, or transmitted in any form, or by any means, electronic, mechanical, photocopying, recording or otherwise without the prior permission in writing of the copyright holders, nor be otherwise circulated in any form or binding or cover other than in which it is published and without a similar condition being imposed on the subsequent publisher.

ISBN 978-1-78091-446-6

Printed and bound in the UK by Copytech (UK) Ltd Peterborough

Contents

Foreword	7
Greg Abbott	8
Bruce Bannister	10
Sam Barkas	12
Bobby Bauld	14
Peter Beagrie	16
Charlie Bicknell	18
Robbie Blake	20
Dickie Bond	22
Irvine Boocock	24
Tommy Cairns	26
Bobby Campbell	28
Robert Campbell	30
Eddie Carr	32
Trevor Cherry	34
Joe Cooke	36
Ian Cooper	38
Terry Dolan	40
Peter Downsborough	42
Donald Duckett	44
Lee Duxbury	46
Roy Ellam	48
Mark Ellis	50
Dave Evans	52
Jock Ewart	54
Tom Flockett	56
Oscar Fox	58
David Fretwell	60
Allan Gilliver	62
David Gray	64
John Hall	66
Tom Hallett	68
Jack Hallows	70
Bobby Ham	72
Joe Hargreaves	74
Derek Hawksworth	76
Stafford Heginbotham	78
John Hendrie	80
George Hinsley	82
Don Hutchins	84
Gerry Ingram	86
David Jackson	88
Peter Jackson	90
Peter Jackson	92
Peter Jackson (manager)	94
Wayne Jacobs	96
Paul Jewell	98
Rod Johnson	100
Chris Kamara	102
Jim Lawlor	104
Jamie Lawrence	106
David Layne	108
Ken Leek	110
Peter Logan	112
Stuart McCall	114
Sean McCarthy	116
John McCole	118
Jimmy McDonald	120
Roy McFarland	122
Andy McGill	124
Jim McLaren	126
David McNiven	128
John Middleton	130
Brian Mitchell	132
Charlie Moore	134
George Mulholland	136
George Murphy	138
Graham Oates	140
Andrew O'Brien	142
Gavin Oliver	144
Ian Ormondroyd	146
Frank O'Rourke	148
Peter O'Rourke	150
Harold Peel	152
Ces Podd	154
Ivor Powell	156
John Reid	158
Julian Rhodes	160
Dean Richards	162
Geoffrey Richmond	164
Arthur Rigby	166
George Robinson	168
Abe Rosenthal	170
Lee Sinnott	172
Geoff Smith	174
Jimmy Speirs	176
Derek Stokes	178
Charlie Storer	180
Bruce Stowell	182
Paul Tomlinson	184
Jack Tordoff	186
Bob Torrance	188
Whelan 'Polly' Ward	190
Dickie Watmough	192
Billy Watson	194
Garry Watson	196
Bobby Webb	198
David Wetherall	200
Jock Whyte	202
George Williamson	204
Dean Windass	206

Acknowledgments

I am grateful to many people for helping me to produce the Bradford City Legends book. First of all, I would like to thank the players I have interviewed, for their patience and co-operation in helping me to record their memories of their careers at Valley Parade. The book is all about them.

I would also like to thank my friend Mick Illingworth for writing the Foreword and for his help and encouragement in producing the book.

I have drawn heavily on the *Bradford City, A Complete Record* published by Breedon in 1988 and written by my friend Terry Frost. For biographies of Bradford City players and their various statistics, this book is invaluable. I am also grateful to Terry for supplying me with statistics of other players not included in his 1988 book.

Other statistics I have taken from the PFA Premier and Football League Players' Records 1946-2005.

I have also used the website jimmy-speirs.co.uk, set up by Andrew Pickles for detailed information about the career of Jimmy Speirs. He was Bradford City's captain when they won the FA Cup in 1911 and scored the vital goal when they beat Newcastle United in the Cup Final replay at Old Trafford.

The book could not have been published without photographs and I am grateful to the *Telegraph & Argus* and their staff, my friends John Dewhirst, John Ashton and David Pendleton for supplying photographs of the players and officials featured in the book. Thank you all.

David Markham

Foreword

by Mick Illingworth

I was delighted to be asked by my friend David Markham to contribute to the legends book of my home-town club, the mighty Bantams. My father introduced me to League football in November 1958 by taking me to Valley Parade, and I was hooked as City beat Rochdale 7–1. I stood on a crate at the front of the Midland Road stand and leaned over the wall getting cold, bruised and filthy with whitewash on my trousers. The dye was cast, and over the years I have witnessed the ups and downs of Bradford City FC, the great comebacks, and I have also been privileged to be entertained by many of the players featured in the book.

I have asked myself 'What is a legend?' Well, in my opinion, it is simple – it is a player who has worn the claret and amber with pride and passion and, more importantly, has shown he had won the hearts of the Valley Parade faithful.

Without doubt, it's a case of cometh the hour, cometh the man, whether playing home or away against Hartlepool or Stockport on a windy January day or gracing the glamour clubs such as Manchester United or Liverpool.

The stories in this book take the reader on a journey into personal memories of their own favourites, the goals they scored, the saves they made or simply the enjoyment they gave over a few games or many years of loyal service.

If you are looking for a book on Bradford City that is full of controversy, disputes and back stabbing then this is not for you. However, if you thirst for an entertaining and interesting look at the legends of City then this is the book you need. I know that David has spent many hours interviewing players to ensure that you, the supporter, will get the feel for the man and his views on his playing career at Valley Parade.

There is enough nostalgia to make pleasant reading for a serious City follower, young or old, and ample pleasantries for the genuine lovers of the greatest game in the world.

Greg Abbott

Date of birth: 14 December 1963

Bradford City record:
Appearances: League 281, FA Cup 15, League Cup 25
Goals: League 38, FA Cup 3, League Cup 6
Debut: 19 February 1983 v Plymouth Argyle

Also played for: Coventry City, Halifax Town, Guiseley, Hull City
Managed: Assistant manager, caretaker manager Carlisle United

A more determined, committed competitor has rarely been seen in a Bradford City shirt than Greg Abbott. Abbott was one of a group of young players who, together at Valley Parade in the early 1980s, not only took City to the Second Division for the first time for 48 years in 1985 but also to the verge of the First Division – now the Premiership – three years later.

Abbott joined City as a right-back on a free transfer from Coventry in 1982 and eventually succeeded City's record appearance holder Ces Podd two years later, as player-manager Trevor Cherry's Third Division Championship team began to take shape.

Now assistant manager at Carlisle United, Abbott recalled 'It was a transformation time at the club. Trevor Cherry was getting rid of the older players and bringing in younger ones, and we went a long way together, culminating in the Play-off defeat against Middlesbrough in 1988 when we just missed out on promotion to the old First Division.

'There was a fantastic team spirit at that time – the whole club seemed to be together. Obviously, there was Stuart McCall and John Hendrie, who were a little bit special, but there was a fantastic work ethic among everyone – it was fantastic to be part of it.

'I think of Martin Singleton, Mark Ellis, Peter Jackson, Dave Evans, Gavin Oliver, Brian Mitchell, John Hawley, Bobby Campbell, Karl Goddard, Chris Withe – they were special times.

'The fire disaster brought us even closer and made us all the more determined to succeed. We felt we were playing for each other and playing for the memory of those who died that day. When I went to Valley Parade with Carlisle at the start of the 2006–07 season, I compared the ground with what I found when I arrived there in 1982, when it was one of the worst in the League. Now, not only is it one of the best in League One but one of the best in the division up from that. I like to think the new ground is a memorial to those who died in the fire.'

It all turned sour for Abbott when John Docherty succeeded Terry Yorath as City manager in March 1990. The club were relegated at the end of that season, and Docherty made changes, bringing in several players with whom he had been associated at his former club Millwall. Abbott felt Docherty split the dressing room with the players he brought in and the spirit that had been developed at Valley Parade. 'I thought John Docherty was a disaster,' said Abbott. 'He altered the whole ethos of the club. It was disappointing, and the club struggled to get back on track until Paul Jewell took over as manager.'

Abbott was looking forward to completing 10 years at Valley Parade and earning a testimonial, but he left after just nine years at the club, for whom he made 281 League appearances and scored 38 goals. 'I was probably too strong in voicing my opinions and the manager was always going to win,' he recalls. 'I lost my appetite for the game.'

Abbott left City in 1991 to join Halifax Town, but after a brief spell at the Shay, where he played 28 League games, he moved to non-League Guiseley for a short time before resurrecting his League career at Hull City. There, as a competitive midfield player, he made 128 League appearances, scoring 16 goals, before retiring in 1995 to move into what is proving to be a successful coaching career.

'I got a bad injury at Halifax, and Guiseley kindly offered me the chance to get back to fitness, and then I got back into League football with Terry Dolan at Hull,' he said 'I loved my time at Hull. I had five years there and met some great people.

'Then, just when I was finishing my career, Ces Podd approached me to do some coaching at Leeds United. I took my coaching badges.

'I worked at the Leeds academy with under-10s through to the under-18s with Brian Kidd, and I had a short spell in charge of the reserves, but all the time I wanted to do senior coaching.

'I turned down the offer to do some short-term coaching with Paul Jewell at Wigan. I was waiting for my own time to go into senior management, and the call came from Neil McDonald [former Newcastle and Everton midfield player] when he took over as manager at Carlisle in the summer of 2006. It is a lovely club, and we have a good spirit and I am really enjoying my coaching.'

Abbott also played a key part in developing the early career of England and Tottenham Hotspur winger Aaron Lennon. 'I coached Aaron in the under-14s in my first season at Leeds United,' said Abbott. 'He is extra special and we still speak to each other now and again.

'In my opinion, he will be one of the best players England has ever had. He was under used in the World Cup, especially with Wayne Rooney not being at full throttle. When he made his World Cup debut I was more excited than I was when I played myself.'

Bruce Bannister

Date of birth: 14 April 1947

Bradford City record:
Appearances: League 208, FA Cup 10, League Cup 10
Goals: League 60, FA Cup 7, League Cup 1
Debut: 4 September 1965 v Colchester United

Also played for: Bristol Rovers, Plymouth Argyle, Hull City, US Dunkerque

Bruce Bannister is undoubtedly one of the best Bradford-born footballers. On the small side, but strong, determined – sometimes fiery – and quick off the mark, Bannister's eye for goal brought him 167 League goals in 523 matches with four clubs during a professional career spanning 14 seasons.

Like his teammates and contemporaries Bruce Stowell and Bobby Ham, Bannister went to Grange School in Bradford, but he began his career as an associated schoolboy with Leeds United. Leeds decided not to offer him a contract and City signed him in June 1963. He became a full-time professional two years later and made his debut in a 2-1 home defeat against Colchester in September 1965, when City's fortunes were at a low ebb, and made seven appearances in his first season when the club had to apply for re-election.

Bannister claimed a regular place the following season – new manager Willie Watson's first campaign – and played a key role when City won promotion under Jimmy Wheeler in 1968-69, scoring one of the goals in the 3-1 win at Darlington in the last match – a match City needed to win to claim the fourth promotion place. He said 'It is successes I remember, and the Darlington game was my first promotion. I joined the club when they were at the bottom of the Fourth Division and left them when they were about 10th in the Third Division, which I felt was an achievement for my home-town club so I was pleased. At Darlington we went 1-0 down, and the players were taken off the field when a fence at the end, where the City fans were standing, collapsed, but we came back and scored three goals to win. It was an exciting night.'

My favourite Bannister goal came the season before, when City missed out on promotion by one place. The home match against Barnsley was heading for a goalless draw when Bannister scored a spectacular last-minute winner with an overhead-kick.

Bannister, who became the team's penalty taker following the departure of penalty king Charlie Rackstraw, continued to be a key member of the team in the Third Division, missing only five matches in 1969-70. He spent the whole of the following season on the transfer list during a long, drawn out dispute over a contract, but he missed only five matches and was leading scorer with 17, which included four goals in a 5-3 win at Mansfield.

Considering his disputes with the club, it was no surprise when Bannister left Valley Parade, and in November 1971 City received a club record £23,000 when he moved to Bristol Rovers, having scored 60 goals in 208 League appearances and eight goals in 20 Cup matches.

At Bristol, Bannister began a successful partnership with Alan Warboys, and they became known as 'smash and grab'. Bannister and Warboys helped Rovers to promotion to the Second Division in 1973-74. By the time he moved to Plymouth Argyle in 1976, he had scored 80 goals in 206 League matches. Bannister teamed up again with Warboys at Hull City before ending his career in the French League with US Dunkerque.

'I had some happy times at Bristol Rovers,' he said. 'Nothing can take away the thrill of scoring a goal and I have that thrill even now after my career is over. Speak to any forward and you will get exactly the same response – just knocking the ball over the line causes this ridiculous thrill.

'We won the Watney Cup in my first year at Bristol and won promotion the year after that. Then I went to Plymouth because former Blackpool goalkeeper Tony Waiters had taken over as manager. He had a style of management like Arsene Wenger at Arsenal, but he fell out with the directors. When he went I quickly left to go to Hull and from there to France. I enjoyed it there and it was interesting to see how they trained. They worked on individual skills all the time, which is why players coming out of France are technically excellent although they are tactically naive.'

Following his retirement, Bannister established a successful business – Sportshoes Unlimited – in Bradford and has moved into mail order. He still keeps in touch with Bradford City and was delighted to turn out at the fundraising match at Valley Parade in May 2004 during the administration crisis.

Sam Barkas

Date of birth: 29 December 1909
Died: 1989

Bradford City record:
Appearances: League 202, FA Cup 14
Goals: League 8, FA Cup 1
Debut: 4 February 1928 v New Brighton

Also played for: Manchester City
Managed: Workington and Wigan Athletic

A study of Bradford City's history reveals that the club has developed few players of genuine international class. In all too many instances, international players who have graced Valley Parade were past their best, with their international days well behind them. However, in Sam Barkas's case the best was yet to come because when he left City for Manchester City he went on to play for England and had the honour of captaining his country.

Barkas joined City as an 18-year-old, and by the time he left seven years later he was established as one of the best left-backs in the old Second Division and ready to move into the top flight. However, such was his affection for the club that he told the *Yorkshire Sports* some 15 years later 'My unhappiest moment in Bradford came when I left after seven delightful seasons. But for my old club being in financial straits, I would have stayed at Valley Parade, my first love. The homely feeling that existed at Valley Parade would have made anybody down in the mouth at leaving, but the club had to keep the flag flying, and if the money they received for my transfer helped to do that I was happy in my unhappiness.'

Barkas worked down the pits before leaving junior club Middle Dock for City after a trial arranged by his brother Ned. He was signed by manager Colin Veitch and made his debut in the 1927–28 season – City's first in Division Three North following their relegation – when he was 18, making just four appearances. However, he played a full part the following campaign as City won the Third Division North Championship. He didn't play his first match until the beginning of November, but he went on to make 26 appearances, mainly at half-back – Billy Watson was still the regular left-back then – and had the satisfaction of scoring the last goal of the season – in a 3–1 home win over South Shields. The significance of that goal was that it was City's 128th of the season – a record for a 42-match programme.

Barkas continued to play mainly at half-back in the first season back in the Second Division, making 33 appearances, ultimately gaining the left-back position, when Watson finally dropped out of the side after 10 years' service at Valley Parade, and then establishing his long-standing partnership with right-back Charlie Bicknell, who had joined the club from Chesterfield. He played in City's side in the top half of the Second Division until the club were forced to sell him in April 1934 to raise some much needed cash – one of several good players allowed to leave Valley Parade in the 1930s. So, Barkas joined Manchester City in a £5,000 deal, having made 216 League and Cup appearances for the Bantams.

While the transfer was unpopular with supporters, it proved to be a good move for Barkas, who won international honours when he left Valley Parade and had the honour of captaining England against Scotland before a record crowd of 149,000 at Hampden Park in 1937. He won five international caps, but it is said that he would have won more England honours but for the competition provided by Arsenal's Eddie Hapgood, and he earned one of his caps at inside-forward when Ray Bowden was injured and was unable to play against Belgium.

Barkas also enjoyed success at the club, playing in Manchester City's First Division Championship side in 1937 and then helping them back into the top flight as Second Division champions in the first season after the war before returning. After his playing days were over, he managed Workington and Wigan Athletic before they became League clubs. He was also licensee of the Sun Inn at Cottingley and worked briefly with Bradford City selling fundraising tickets.

England manager Alf Ramsey, who masterminded England's 1966 World Cup triumph, described Barkas as a modern player and, although he refused to elaborate on that observation when I wrote to him some years later, I presume by that he meant that as a full-back Barkas preferred to play the ball out of defence, finding a teammate with a pass at a time, when full-backs saw themselves purely as defenders and the normal procedure was to win the ball in the tackle from the winger they were marking and clear the ball over the halfway line to be picked up by more skilful or creative players.

Barkas was so skilful – comfortable on the ball to use modern terminology – that he sometimes played at left-half or inside-left – nowadays midfield positions – and he would have fitted perfectly into the modern game where the emphasis is on skill rather than strength.

Many years after his career ended he was still feted at Maine Road, where he had a sponsors' lounge named after him and enjoyed being taken to watch his old club. He also maintained connections with Bradford City, and the then chief scout Maurice Lindley, who made his name as chief scout at Leeds United. Barkas used him to watch local matches, and he was the one who spotted striker Ian Ormondroyd playing for local Bradford sides Manningham Mills and Thackley.

Sadly, Sam died in December 1989 three weeks short of his 80th birthday.

Bobby Bauld

Date of birth: 14 March 1902

Bradford City record:
Appearances: League 217, FA Cup 10
Goals: League 34, FA Cup 1
Debut: 27 August 1927 v Ashington

Also played for: Glencraig, Raith Rovers, Dundee United, Chesterfield

Bobby Bauld, front row, centre, with the ball, in the Third Division North Championship-winning side of 1928-29.

Scotsman Bobby Bauld was a key signing as City began to rebuild their side after their relegation from the Second Division in 1927. He settled in at left-half – a left side midfield role in modern football – making 227 League and Cup appearances – 217 in the League in eight seasons at Valley Parade. He also possessed a terrific shot, particularly from free-kicks – and scored 35 League and Cup goals during his valuable service with the club.

Bauld began his career with home-town junior club Glencraig and, after an unsuccessful trial with Tottenham Hotspur, he signed as a professional with Raith Rovers. However, it was with another Scottish League club, Dundee United, that Bauld established himself as a player of substance. He arrived at Tannadice as an inside-forward in 1923 before being converted into a left-half, and the following season he played a key role in Dundee United's Second Division Championship triumph.

Then, after scoring an impressive 50 goals in 150 appearances, Bauld surprised everyone when he moved to England to join City. He was one of several significant signings made in the 1927 close season as the club tried to recover from relegation from the Second Division. He made his debut and scored from the penalty spot in the first match of the season – a 2-2 draw at Ashington – and he played in 24 League matches, scoring seven goals as City finished sixth in their first season of Third Division North football.

Bauld played his part the following season as the club returned to Division Two as champions with eight goals in 22 appearances, sharing the left-half position with Sam Barkas. He continued to play regularly for the next five seasons as City established themselves as a good Second Division club without being able to make the breakthrough to the top flight, missing only three matches in each of the 1931-32 and 1932-33 campaigns. However, he managed only five matches as City began to struggle in 1934-35, and at the end of the season he signed for Chesterfield, but he played only twice in the Chesterfield team that won the Third Division North Championship the following season and retired.

His son Phil followed him into professional football and signed for Wolves in 1948 and also had spells with Clyde, Plymouth and Aldershot.

Peter Beagrie

Date of birth: 28 November 1965

Bradford City record:
Appearances: League 131, FA Cup 6, League Cup 9
Goals: League 20, League Cup 3
Debut: 9 August 1997 v Stockport

Also played for: Middlesbrough, Sheffield United, Stoke City, Everton, Sunderland, Manchester City, Everton (loan), Wigan Athletic (loan), Scunthorpe United, Grimsby Town

Having narrowly escaped relegation in 1997 in their first season back in the Second Division, Bradford City were in urgent need of some quality signings to consolidate their place in the higher Division. None turned out better than Peter Beagrie – a £50,000 capture from Manchester City – who was to play a key role in City's promotion to the Premiership two years later. The skilful winger, who could create and sometimes score goals, became a firm favourite with the Valley Parade crowd, not least when he celebrated his goals with a trademark somersault.

When he arrived at Valley Parade, Beagrie had been out of action for nearly two years with a troublesome and complicated knee injury, which had required an operation, but he showed no signs of any injury problems in his four years at Valley Parade.

Not surprisingly, Beagrie pinpoints what he describes as 'an amazing game' at Wolves in May 1999. It was the last match of the season, and City had to win to be sure of automatic promotion. He said 'From the middle of the season we fancied going to Wolves for the last match if we needed points for promotion because defensively they took chances. We were really good at going forward and we were the best team for scoring goals; our 4-4-2 formation was made for goals. We went a goal down, and then I scored an equaliser to put us back in the game. I remember I took the ball off Kevin Muscat and my shot took a deflection on its way into the net.' City then went 3-1 up, and Beagrie had the chance to make it 4-1 but saw his penalty saved. Then Wolves pulled a goal back before hitting the post in some tense closing stages before City won 3-2 to make sure of automatic promotion. 'It was a great penalty save from Mike Stowell to deny me,' said Beagrie, 'and, although they pulled a goal back and hit the post we got what we deserved. Stuart McCall and myself were in tears after the game. We were both 35 or 36 and it meant a lot to us.'

Having gained promotion to the top level, City's challenge was how to stay there. Beagrie said 'Coming to Valley Parade was a shock to the system for the big boys. We respected the big teams, but we never feared them. Dean Windass, David Wetherall, Gunnar Halle and Dean Saunders were seasoned pros with a work ethic, who would run and run. We had quality on the ball, never shirked a tackle and created chances, and we were rewarded with a win to stay up in our final game with Liverpool. Then there was Stuart McCall. I played with Stuart at Everton – we are both winners – and he did a fantastic job – his drive, direction, sometimes unspectacular work gave myself and Robbie Blake freedom – we were always on the ball, but only because of the service we received from Stuart McCall, Jamie Lawrence and Gareth Whalley. They helped us to get forward and gave us a bit more freedom.

'The club would not allow me to go to Sheffield United, so I went on loan to Wigan and helped them into the Play-offs, but Reading beat us. I had a few options when I left Bradford in the summer – to play in the USA, to play or coach with Ajax or in Cape Town – but I went to Scunthorpe where my former Middlesbrough teammate Brian Laws was manager.'

Beagrie became involved with coaching and scouting as well as being a regular player, helping Scunthorpe to promotion from Coca Cola League Two in 2004–05. Twelve months later he stepped down a division to join their Lincolnshire rivals Grimsby Town, but three months into the new season he decided to retire with a back injury and concentrate on a career with Sky TV and ITV. For the last two years of his playing career he had been developing a career in television, and when he announced his retirement he signed a two-year contract with Sky.

His decision to retire brought to an end a 24-year career that began with his home-town club Middlesbrough and continued at Sheffield United, Stoke City, Everton and Manchester City before he resurrected his career at Valley Parade. In all, he made more than 600 League appearances and scored more than 80 goals.

Charlie Bicknell

Date of birth: 6 November 1905
Died: 1994

Bradford City record:
Appearances: League 240, FA Cup 14
Goals: League 2
Debut: 30 August 1930 v Charlton Athletic

Also played for: Chesterfield and West Ham United
Managed: Bedford Town

Consistency was the hallmark of Charlie Bicknell in a remarkably long career spanning more than 20 years. The strong and powerful right-back, named 'Bicknell the bulwark' at Bradford City, played 240 League matches in nearly six seasons after joining them from Chesterfield in 1930, including a run of 224 consecutive appearances, many of them as full-back partner to Sam Barkas.

After missing a match at Preston in November 1930, Bicknell began his extraordinary run of consecutive appearances, which only ended when he was transferred to West Ham in March 1936. A natural leader, he was captain at Valley Parade in his last two seasons there, and he became the first West Ham skipper to lift a major trophy when he helped them to win the 1940 War Cup Final at Wembley by beating Blackburn Rovers 1–0.

Bicknell was born at Pye Bridge near Chesterfield and was a miner in the Derbyshire coalfields before he joined Chesterfield from local side New Tipton Ivanhoe. He played the 1927–28 season as an amateur before signing professional forms, and he spent two more years with Chesterfield, for whom he made 85 League and Cup appearances before joining City in March 1930 for £600, when Peter O'Rourke was in his second spell as manager. The club have made few better signings.

Writing affectionately about his Valley Parade career some 12 years after he left City, Bicknell told the *Yorkshire Sports* 'The biggest and happiest moment of my career at Valley Parade came when I was made City's skipper. It made me feel I had really made the grade and had the confidence of both directors and manager.

'Besides that, we had a fine set of lads in every way, and I was proud to captain them on the field. It remains a happy memory with me now that I have left big football.

'My unhappiest moment at Bradford was when I was transferred to West Ham, the reason being that I had been so happy and comfortable there in every way that I was sorry to leave, but I had to look to the future.

'The years I spent at Bradford were among my happiest memories because I made such good friends there, and I was sorry to leave.'

Bicknell made his West Ham debut in a 4–1 home win over Newcastle on 21 March 1936 and continued the consistency he had shown at Valley Parade by missing only one match in two and a half seasons up to the outbreak of the war. He was an ever present in 1937–38 and missed only one match the following season. He was 34 when war broke out, but his enthusiasm for the game remained undimmed, and he continued to play regularly in regional League and Cup football during the war while serving in the Police Special Constabulary. His 200-plus wartime appearances for West Ham are a club record.

Although he began the 1946–47 season as captain when League football resumed after the war, Bicknell was then 41 and this turned out to be his last campaign. He managed a further 19 matches, his last appearance being at Leicester on 4 January 1947, and he was released at the end of the season, having made 149 League and Cup appearances, 137 being in the League.

So ended a remarkable Football League career, but Bicknell continued in the game and became player-manager of Bedford Town in the Southern League while working in the local electricity works. He died in Cambridgeshire in September 1994 aged 88.

Robbie Blake

Date of birth: 4 March 1976

Bradford City record:
Appearances: League 153, FA Cup 7, League 11
Goals: League 40, FA Cup 1, League Cup 4
Debut: 29 March 1997 v Portsmouth

Also played for: Darlington, Nottingham Forest (loan), Burnley, Birmingham City, Leeds United

Robbie Blake played a significant part in Bradford City's rise to the Premiership, forming one of their best striking partnerships in modern times alongside the club's first £1 million signing Lee Mills. The two players scored 42 goals between them as City made sure of the second automatic promotion place with a thrilling 3–2 win at Wolves on the final day of the 1998–99 season.

Blake also played a significant part in the club's two Premiership seasons before moving to Burnley for £1 million in January 2002 after a loan spell at Nottingham Forest, as City began the downward slide towards the first of their two administrations. He was one of several shrewd signings made by Chris Kamara during his two-year spell as manager at Valley Parade – Darren Moore and Peter Beagrie were among the others – when he joined City from Darlington on transfer deadline day in March 1997 a few weeks after his 21st birthday, but it was Kamara's successor Paul Jewell who reaped the full benefits of the striker's talents.

Blake, who has been involved in three £1 million-plus transfers – to Burnley, Birmingham City and present club Leeds United – said 'The move to Bradford City came out of the blue. They were struggling in the old First Division – now the Championship – and I played in a couple of games as we survived, but I got more chances after we stayed up.

'The promotion season was a fantastic season not only for the manager Paul Jewell but also for the players. We made a bad start, but we then started on an amazing run and gained automatic promotion on the last day of the season with a 3–2 win at Wolves.

'You couldn't top the Wolves game. That was a very special day and to score one of the goals topped it all off for me. We went 1–0 down and we heard from our fans that our rivals Ipswich were beating Sheffield United, but we showed great character throughout the season and to beat Wolves on their own ground and avoid going into the Play-offs was a great achievement.'

However, that momentous season in Bradford City's history did not start well either for Blake or the team. He recalls 'I was sent off against Portsmouth on the last day of the 1997–98 season, and so I missed the first three matches of the new campaign. The club had brought in Lee Mills and Isaiah Rankin, but Isaiah got injured and I got my chance against Oxford United, and we did well. Paul Jewell stayed with me; we went on a good run and I finished the season scoring 19 goals, while Lee Mills scored 25. It was one of those partnerships that worked really well. We hit it off straightaway. I was more of a link man and Lee Mills more of a target man.

'To play in the Premiership was fantastic, especially to stay up in the first season. To come to Valley Parade was an eye opener for some of the big clubs, and we beat big teams like Arsenal and Newcastle on our own ground, and to survive by beating Liverpool on the last day of the season was fantastic. I believe we survived because of our home form, which was pretty good. No one expected us to beat Liverpool at home, but David Wetherall put us in front early and we managed to win.

'It is a shame to see how Bradford City have declined. It is a club that is close to me as regards my progression in football and there are a lot of people I have to thank. The club went downhill from the day Paul Jewell left at the end of the first Premiership season, but they still have potential.

'After Paul Jewell left, the club went a little too big in trying to bring in big name players and spending a lot of money. I don't think it was the right thing to do – there was too much money being taken out of the club. Players like Benito Carbone and Dan Petrescu were used to big clubs and Bradford City was a shock to them. The club brought in about 15 new players and it was obvious we were not going to click straightaway. That was the gamble chairman Geoffrey Richmond took, but it backfired and the club have not recovered.'

Blake scored 45 goals in 171 League and Cup appearances at Valley Parade before moving to Burnley and said 'Burnley was a good move. I went there with a hernia problem so I didn't start well, but it was a good time and my spell at Turf Moor further progressed my career and then to get a move to Birmingham was another great move for me.

'Paul Jewell tried to sign me for Wigan Athletic, but I went to Birmingham for £1.2 million in January 2005. I scored on my debut against Southampton in the Premiership and I always figured either in the starting line-up or on the bench. I got my fair share of games there, but at the end of the season manager Steve Bruce was in a situation where he had to release players to bring in new ones. So, I joined Leeds United for £1 million. In my first season Leeds were trying to get back in the Premiership and we managed to reach the Play-off Final only to be beaten by Watford.

However, Leeds were relegated to League One for the first time in their history in May 2007 and went into administration. So, during the summer Blake re-joined Burnley two and a half years after leaving them.

Dickie Bond

Date of birth: 1883
Died: April 1955

Bradford City record:
Appearances: League 301, FA Cup 31
Goals: League 60, FA Cup 12
Debut: 1 September 1909 v Manchester United

Also played for: Preston North End, Blackburn Rovers, Lancaster City

There is little doubt that the most famous player to wear the claret and amber was Dickie Bond. The England international was one of the best – if not the best – outside-rights in the early 1900s, but when he joined City from Preston North End in May 1909 his fitness was in doubt because of a knee injury. The club doctor examined Bond's knee and, despite his doubts, he advised the club to take a chance, and Bond joined City for a bargain fee of £950.

Dodgy knee or not, Bond played in 332 League and FA Cup matches, scoring 73 goals in a 13-year career at Valley Parade, interrupted by war when League football was suspended for four seasons. All his 301 League appearances were in the top division, and he also played 28 wartime matches, scoring 10 goals. Even after he left City in 1922, he still played for one season at Blackburn Rovers before joining non-League Lancaster City for a final campaign in 1923, by which time he was 40.

Bond was born at Garstang in 1883 and began playing football with the Royal Artillery before signing for Preston as a professional in 1902. At Deepdale, he gained a Second Division Championship medal in 1904, and two years later he was a member of the team that finished runners-up in the First Division. He made his City debut at the start of the 1909-10 season and missed only two matches, as well as scoring six goals, as the club finished a creditable seventh. He also regained his England place, playing in all three home internationals against Scotland, Wales and Ireland, who played as one team in those days.

Besides being an outstanding player, Bond was also a fiery, forthright, often outspoken character, who was no stranger to being in trouble now and again, and his indiscipline cost him a place in City's FA Cup Final team the following season when he was suspended twice. His two suspensions, one by the club, the other by the FA, were also the main reasons he missed 12 of City's 38 League matches – the season they achieved their highest-ever League placing – fifth in the top division.

Bond resumed his regular place in the side the following season, missing only four matches and one of seven FA Cup games as City reached the quarter-finals. His consistency continued until League football was suspended in 1915 because of World War One and he formed a fine understanding with his inside-forward partner Oscar Fox as City continued to be a good class First Division team.

He served with the Bradford Pals during World War One and was held prisoner by the Germans for nearly three years. They were clearly delighted to capture such a famous prisoner and displayed a banner proclaiming 'We've captured Dickie Bond'. When City played at Arsenal in 1920 Bond laid a wreath at the newly-created cenotaph in memory of his friends and teammates who died in the war.

Bond was made club captain after the war and played for three more seasons as City battled to keep their First Division status and received a record £700 benefit after a match against Newcastle in February 1920. He made 473 League appearances with 96 goals when he retired. Bond became a publican when his playing career was over. He died in April 1955, aged 71.

Irvine Boocock

Date of birth: 1890
Died: 11 November 1941

Bradford City record:
Appearances: League 169, FA Cup 15
Goals: League 1
Debut: 5 March 1910 v Aston Villa

Also played for: Darlington

Cleckheaton-born Irvine Boocock was one of Bradford City's most reliable players either side of World War One, making 169 League appearances – all in the First Division – in nine peacetime seasons at Valley Parade. He made his debut against Aston Villa in March 1910, but it took him three seasons to gain a regular place in the side. Boocock made only one appearance in 1910-11, when City won the FA Cup and finished fifth in Division One, but he played 10 games in 1911-12 after Cup Final left-back David Taylor was transferred to Burnley. He was a regular player in the three seasons before League football was suspended for World War One, playing with full-back partner Robert Campbell, and he missed only one match in 1913-14. Such was his outstanding form that season that he was rewarded by the Football League selectors, who chose him for the League against the Scottish League at Turf Moor in March 1914, and later that year he played against the Irish League at West Bromwich Albion and the Southern League at Arsenal's new Highbury ground.

Boocock also appeared in two unofficial matches for the Football League XI against a Scottish League XI at Shawfield Park, Glasgow, in April 1914 and against Scotland at Goodison Park in May 1916 in a 'Grand Military International', by which time he was in the armed forces.

Like many of his generation, Boocock's career was badly disrupted by the war when League football was suspended for four seasons. He was at his peak when war broke out and, having gained League representative honours just before the war, whether he would have progressed into the international side, we will never know.

Boocock was 29 when League football resumed after the war, but after playing regularly in the first half of the 1919-20 season he played only twice in the second half of the campaign as Alex Doolan took the left-back spot. However, Doolan was transferred to Preston just before the following season began, and Boocock seized his chance, missing only one match, while full-back partner Freddie Potts missed only three, as City continued their battle to hang on to their First Division status.

However, in the summer of 1921 City paid a club-record fee to Airdrieonians for Billy Watson, and he was the club's regular left-back for the next 10 years. Boocock played only twice in 1921-22 and left Valley Parade as City were relegated and joined Darlington in the Third Division North, leaving memories of a fine career which featured 169 First Division appearances and 15 in the FA Cup, but only one goal. He also made 64 wartime appearances.

Boocock was also a good cricketer and played in the Bradford League for Cleckheaton, Eccleshill and East Bierley. He was involved for 30 years at Cleckheaton as a player, steward and groundsman.

Tommy Cairns

Date of birth: 1890
Died: 1967

Bradford City record:
Appearances: League 135, FA Cup 11
Goals: League 32, FA Cup 4
Debut: 27 August 1927 v Ashington

Also played for: Burnbank Athletic, Larkhall Thistle, Bristol City, Peebles Rovers, St Johnstone, Glasgow Rangers

Tommy Cairns

Tommy Cairns, second row centre (seated), with the ball between his feet, in this 1930–31 team photograph. In the team are also Sam Barkas, Bobby Bauld and Charlie Bicknell, who are all featured in this book.

Tommy Cairns's best years were behind him when he joined Bradford City in June 1927 from Glasgow Rangers for a bargain £600 just over a month after they were relegated from the Second Division to the Third Division North, but what a valuable acquisition he turned out to be. For, by the time he retired five years later, a few months short of his 42nd birthday, the Scottish international inside-forward had helped City back to the Second Division as Third Division North Champions – as captain – and played his part in establishing them as a good class Division Two team, making 146 League and Cup appearances and scoring 36 goals.

He had slowed up a good deal by the time he arrived at Valley Parade – in fact, the players used to nickname him 'Speedy' – but his skill and experience were hugely valuable at a critical period in the club's history and left supporters marvelling at what a wonderful player he must have been at his peak.

Cairns began his playing career with Burnbank Athletic and won a Scottish Junior Cup-winners' medal with them in 1911 before joining Larkhall Thistle.

After a short spell in the English League with Bristol City, Cairns returned to Scotland and played for Peebles Rovers before St Johnstone signed him in 1913. He then moved to Rangers and, in a 14-year spell with them, he gained seven Scottish League Championship medals, two Scottish Cup runners'-up medals and eight full international caps as well as an appearance in a Victory international and six games for the Scottish League.

Little could it have been anticipated that when he joined City aged 37 that he would play for five seasons at Valley Parade, and he was the oldest player to turn out for City in peacetime football.

He later worked as a Scottish-based scout for Arsenal and died in 1967.

Bobby Campbell

Date of birth: 13 September 1956

Bradford City record:
Appearances: League 274, FA Cup 12, League Cup 24
Goals: League 121, FA Cup 5, League Cup 11
Debut: 12 January 1980 v Peterborough United

Also played for: Aston Villa, Halifax Town (twice), Huddersfield Town (twice), Sheffield United, Vancouver Whitecaps, Brisbane City, Derby County, Wigan Athletic

Legend is an overworked word in football, but it surely applies to Bobby Campbell. He is Bradford City's all-time record goalscorer with 121 goals in 274 League appearances in almost eight seasons between 1980 and 1986, breaking Frank O'Rourke's record of 88 League goals set before World War One. He also scored 22 goals in Cup matches, making a total of 143 goals in 320 appearances for the club.

It is a magnificent record that has made Campbell one of the most popular players in the modern era. However, it was not just his top-class goalscoring record that made Bobby such a big favourite. His larger-than-life character on and off the field and his fearless attitude and willingness to endure pain for the Bantams cause made him an iconic figure at Valley Parade.

The Northern Ireland striker had a bad boy reputation when he arrived at Valley Parade in January 1980, having been sacked by Halifax Town for 'persistent misconduct' the previous May, but, although he liked a drink or two, none of his three City managers could have any complaints about his commitment to the club.

After being sacked by Halifax, Campbell went to Australia to play for Brisbane City, but he arrived back in England looking for a club, and City manager George Mulhall decided to give him a month's trial with a stern warning as to his future conduct. He need not have worried as Campbell was an instant success and played in every game to the end of the season, scoring eight goals in 21 matches as City frustratingly missed promotion on goal average.

Campbell was top scorer for the first time with 19 goals in 41 appearances in 1980-81, but it was a disappointing season as City suffered a hangover following their failed promotion effort. He played a key role in the following campaign when they won promotion from the Fourth Division under new manager Roy McFarland. He established a good partnership in his first two seasons with David McNiven, and the partnership blossomed in a spectacular way during the promotion campaign. They missed only one match between them as Campbell top scored with 24 goals in 45 matches, while ever-present McNiven notched 19. Their combined total of 43 goals made a huge contribution to a successful season.

Campbell did even better the following season, scoring 25 in 40 appearances, but then came an unexpected break in his Valley Parade career as the club faced a financial crisis that almost put them out of business.

City went into receivership in the summer of 1983 owing £400,000 and could not refuse an £70,000 offer for Campbell from Derby County just before the 1983-84 season. After four miserable months at Derby, he returned to City, first on loan and then for a £35,000 fee, to spark a spectacular revival in their fortunes.

They won only one of their first 14 matches, but soon after Campbell came back they began a record-breaking run of 10 consecutive League wins that rescued their season. Campbell formed a successful striking partnership with John Hawley, who ended the season as leading scorer with 22 League goals.

Campbell was also leading scorer the following season with 23 League goals as the Bantams were crowned Third Division Champions. The Valley Parade fire tragedy turned City's triumph into tragedy and there followed a difficult season in which they played home matches at three different venues. Despite this handicap, City managed to finish a creditable 13th, with Campbell finishing joint top scorer with 10 goals – the same as John Hendrie and Greg Abbott.

He made a good start to the new campaign, scoring three goals in the first seven matches, including one in the famous 2-0 win over Leeds United at Odsal, but then manager Trevor Cherry shocked City supporters by selling him to Wigan Athletic for £25,000. He scored 27 goals in 69 League matches at Wigan, playing as striking partner with future City manager Paul Jewell before retiring two years later having scored 179 career League goals in 477 appearances.

Belfast-born Campbell began his career as an apprentice with Aston Villa in 1972 before moving on loan to Halifax Town for the first of two spells at The Shay. He was then transferred to Huddersfield Town before moving to Sheffield United. He had a brief spell at Huddersfield followed, by a short spell in Canadian football with Vancouver, before he joined Halifax for a second time.

The Northern Ireland FA imposed a life ban on him for misconduct during a youth tour in Switzerland as a 17-year-old, but Roy McFarland persuaded them to lift the ban in 1982 and Campbell played against Scotland before making a substitute appearance against Wales. He also went to Spain for the World Cup, but was never fit to play.

Robert Campbell

Date of birth: 1882
Died: 13 March 1931

Bradford City record:
Appearances: League 223, FA Cup 24
Goals: League 1
Debut: 1 September 1906 v Leeds City

Also played for: Partick Thistle, Glasgow Rangers, Millwall Athletic

Big kicking right-back Robert Campbell shared in two major Bradford City triumphs in his nine seasons at Valley Parade. The Scottish-born player was a key part of City's Second Division Championship-winning team in 1907–08 before helping them to win the FA Cup three years later, which marked the height of his career.

Born at Lugar Boswell, Campbell established himself in Scotland with Partick Thistle and Glasgow Rangers before moving to England, joining Southern League club Millwall Athletic in the 1905 close season. He played one season with them before joining City in May 1906, where he made 29 League appearances as partner to left-back Fred Farren as manager Peter O'Rourke gradually began to put together a team ready for an assault on the Division Two Championship the following season.

City finished fifth that season but led from the front in the following campaign as another Scot, centre-forward Frank O'Rourke, signed just before the end of the previous season and made his mark by top scoring with 21 goals and Wallace Smith scored 20. Their reward for winning the Second Division title was their first continental tour, and Campbell was a popular 'tourist', with the Belgians nicknaming him 'L'aimie' – the friendly one – because of his perpetual smile.

Campbell, again partnering Farren, made 30 League appearances and rose to the challenge of the top flight with 25 matches the following season, while Peter O'Rourke was forced to make several changes as City successfully fought to preserve their First Division status, which they duly did by beating Manchester United 1–0 in a tense last match.

City gradually established themselves in the top division, finishing seventh in 1909–10 with Campbell a key part of the team, missing only five League matches, and although he played only 23 matches the following season, as the club achieved fifth place, their highest ever placing, crucially he played in all seven Cup games, including the Cup Final matches against Newcastle United at Crystal Palace and Old Trafford.

City's 0–0 draw at Crystal Palace was a tremendous defensive effort on a blustery day in London, which earned them a replay at Old Trafford. In the replay they also denied Newcastle after skipper Jimmy Speirs had scored what proved to be the winning goal, and Campbell played a prominent part in those sterling defensive displays. There were no overlapping full-backs or wing-backs who joined in the attack in those days, and Campbell was renowned for his huge clearances and the crowd cheered when he kicked the ball upfield to safety.

Campbell also played in seven Cup matches the following season, when City made a valiant effort to retain the Cup, only to be knocked out in the quarter-final by the eventual winners Barnsley after two dramatic replays. He continued to play regularly until League football was suspended during World War One, after making 223 League appearances and playing in 24 Cup games, making 247 in all, his eight seasons covering the outstanding period in the club's long history.

Campbell, who was such a good cricketer that he played professional with the Clydesdale club, returned to Scotland after his retirement, but sadly he died aged only 49.

Eddie Carr

Date of birth: 3 October 1917
Died: June 1998

Bradford City record:
Appearances: League 94, FA Cup 5
Goals: League 49, FA Cup 7
Debut: 29 October 1949 v Crewe Alexandra

Also played for: Arsenal, Huddersfield Town, Newport County, Darlington
Managed: Darlington

Eddie Carr was not the most energetic or hardworking player, but as a goal poacher he had few equals in and around the six-yard area. His impressive goalscoring record tells its own story – 49 goals in 94 League matches in his four seasons at Valley Parade, including five hat-tricks – a club record he shares with Jack Deakin, who scored a remarkable 51 League and FA Cup goals in 69 appearances in three seasons leading up to World War Two. For good measure, Carr also scored seven goals in five FA Cup games.

Like so many players of his generation, Carr's career was ruined by the war. When the war started he was one month short of his 22nd birthday. When League football resumed in 1946 he was 28.

Carr's career started well. He was playing with non-League Margate as a 17-year-old when he a got a big break in 1935 by joining Arsenal. The 1930s were one of the most successful periods of the Gunners' illustrious history and, not surprisingly, Carr found it difficult to break into that star-studded side, but he deputised for the injured Ted Drake in 11 matches in 1937–38 and proved to be a lucky mascot. Arsenal were unbeaten in those matches, Carr scoring seven goals as Arsenal won another League Championship.

Carr guested for several clubs during the war, including Bradford Park Avenue and Newcastle United, and in July 1945 he signed for Huddersfield Town. After only two League appearances in the first season after the war, he joined Newport County in October 1946 and averaged one goal for every two matches over a three-year period. Carr was leading scorer with 19 goals in his first season, but he could not stop Newport being relegated from the Third Division South. He continued to score regularly for the Welsh club and was joint leading scorer the following season and helped Newport to the fifth round of the FA Cup in the 1948–49 season. By the time City signed him for a four-figure fee in October 1949 he had scored 48 goals in 98 League matches for Newport, including three hat-tricks.

Having suffered the indignity of having to apply for re-election for the first time in their history the season before, City were desperate for a good start to the new campaign, but they were short of goals so manager David Steele turned to two of the most experienced forwards around at that time, signing Carr from Newport and the former Huddersfield Town player Bill Price from Hull City within a couple of weeks of each other.

Maybe both of them were past their peak, but they knew their way to goal. Significantly, both scored on their respective League debuts. Carr was on the mark in his first match – a 2–2 draw at Crewe – and Price scored from the penalty spot in his first game the following week – a 3–2 home win over Barrow when Carr also scored again. In fact, Carr scored in his first four games. They also enjoyed themselves the following week when City met non-League club Fleetwood at Valley Parade in the first round of the FA Cup in front of a crowd of 14,257. City were in the bottom half of the Third Division North, but they thrashed the Lancashire Combination side 9–0 with Carr scoring four goals and Price, three – one of them a penalty.

Although Carr's goals dried up after that, he came good at the end of the season, scoring three goals in the last five matches. At the same time, Price finished the season as the leading scorer with 12 League goals in 25 matches as City won three of their last four matches, including a 6–0 thrashing of Southport on Easter Monday and a 5–2 win over Accrington Stanley in the last match, which enabled them to avoid having to seek re-election for the second season in a row. Carr and Price continued their fruitful partnership the following season, Price again finishing as top scorer with 15 in 21 matches while Carr scored 13 in 22 games.

However, Carr saved the best until what proved to be his last season – 1952–53. He finished the season as leading scorer with 20 goals in 28 League matches, including an extraordinary eight goals in three matches over five days of the Easter holiday weekend, when City scored no fewer than 15 goals. Carr scored a hat-trick in the 4–4 draw at Workington on Good Friday, two more when they beat Workington 4–0 in the return match at Valley Parade the following day and another hat-trick when they thrashed Carlisle United 7–2 at home on Easter Tuesday. The first goal of his hat-trick against Carlisle was his 100th League goal, and he received a rapturous reception from the 12,836 crowd.

Carr left Valley Parade that summer to join Darlington, but he couldn't gain a regular place there, and the following July he was appointed head trainer, retiring as a player with the impressive record of 104 League goals in 213 appearances and 13 FA Cup goals in 13 matches. He became caretaker manager at Darlington in June 1960 and was appointed permanent manager five months later. After four years in charge, he was replaced by player Lol Morgan. He then spent five years as manager of the famous north-east non-League club Tow Law Town. Carr also scouted for Newcastle United from 1969 to 1974. He died in June 1998 aged 80.

Trevor Cherry

Date of birth: 23 February 1948

Bradford City record:
Appearances: League 92, FA Cup 4, League Cup 6
Debut: 27 December 1982 v Preston North End

Also played for: Huddersfield Town, Leeds United
Managed: Bradford City

Trevor Cherry broke the mould of 48 years of lower division football when he guided City to the Third Division Championship in 1984–85. Supporters, who had been brought up on a diet of Third and Fourth Division fooball, had almost despaired of seeing Second Division football again, but Cherry gave them that after a memorable season that ended in the Valley Parade fire tragedy when 56 lost their lives.

The former England defender joined the club as player-manager in December 1982 from Leeds United after Roy McFarland had left City to return to Derby County.

McFarland had guided City to promotion from the Fourth Division the season before, and Cherry, aided by inspirational coach and former Leeds teammate Terry Yorath, set about building another promotion team to take the club to a level they had not enjoyed since they were relegated to the Third Division North in 1937.

Chairman Bob Martin and his board acted quickly and decisively to fill the gap left by McFarland's controversial departure, and the choice of Cherry, another former England defender, proved to be an inspired appointment.

Few managers have faced such difficult off-the-field problems – a financial crisis that plunged the club into receivership and the horror of the fire disaster that forced the team to play away from their own ground for 18 months – but he overcame them all while continuing his playing career, before injury forced him into premature retirement.

So, after watching his new team beat Mansfield in the FA Cup second round after a replay at Valley Parade, Cherry took his place in the next match and made 28 consecutive appearances to the end of the season, while Yorath concentrated on coaching. It made for a near perfect arrangement, but Cherry faced unprecedented problems in the first 12 months of his management.

On the field, City went 10 League and Cup matches until their first win under their new manager, but Cherry managed to guide them to a respectable mid-table place in their first season back in the Third Division. Off the field, one of City's floodlights blew down in the February gales, and it became obvious that storm clouds of a financial nature were looming as well. The clouds burst in June when City were placed into receivership owing £400,000. For two months the future of the club hung on a thread before Stafford Heginbotham and Jack Tordoff came together to save the club.

Money was tight in the new season, and City won only one of their first 15 matches as gates dipped below the 3,000 mark. Then striker Bobby Campbell returned from Derby County, where he had been sold during the summer, and City embarked on a record-breaking 10-match winning run and finished a creditable seventh.

Cherry, who continued to lead by example, missing only two matches, made two crucial signings – Dave Evans and John Hendrie – as he set about building a promotion team, and City not only won promotion, but romped to the Third Division Championship before the fire tragedy turned triumph into disaster.

Cherry switched to right-back to accommodate Evans in the centre of the defence, but unfortunately he was injured in the home match against Millwall in November and played only five more matches that season before announcing his retirement, having made 679 League appearances for three West Yorkshire clubs – Huddersfield Town, Leeds United and City.

After the fire, City faced life in the demanding Second Division under the handicap of having to play their matches at Leeds United, Huddersfield Town and Bradford's Odsal Stadium, while decisions were being made about the rebuilding of Valley Parade. At the same time, money was in short supply for team strengthening. Nonetheless, City finished in 13th place, which was a major achievement for Cherry and the players.

Cherry lost right-hand man Terry Yorath during the 1986 close season. Yorath became manager of Swansea and was succeeded by youth-team coach Terry Dolan. Dolan then replaced Cherry when he was surprisingly sacked seven months later – three weeks after Valley Parade re-opened.

That proved to be the end of his football career that began with home-town club Huddersfield, whom he captained to the Second Division title in 1970. He moved to Leeds when Town were relegated two years later and won a League Championship medal and appeared in FA Cup and European Finals during 10 years at Elland Road.

Joe Cooke

Date of birth: 15 February 1955

Bradford City record:
Appearances: League 266, FA Cup 19, League Cup 17
Goals: League 68, FA Cup 4, League Cup 7
Debut: 11 September 1971 v Chesterfield

Also played for: Peterborough United, Oxford United, Exeter City, Rochdale, Wrexham

Versatile Joe Cooke was a valuable player for City during two spells in the 1970s and 1980s, playing more than 300 League and Cup matches for the club at a time when black players were still trying to establish themselves in English football.

Born on the Leeward Island of Dominica, Cooke came to England as a child and attended Buttershaw School in Bradford. He quickly made his mark in schoolboy football and joined City as an associate schoolboy in July 1970 after some impressive appearances for Bradford Boys. Big and strong for his age, he made his debut as a substitute in a home match against Chesterfield in September 1971 as a 16-year-old, and he became a full-time professional at the end of that season.

Cooke made his mark as a powerfully-built central-defender, but such was his strong presence that City successfully used him as a centre-forward in 1975–76 when they reached the FA Cup quarter-final and in the following season when they won promotion to the Third Division. He scored 22 Leagues goals in 42 appearances in 1975–76 and scored two goals in the FA Cup and 17 goals in 40 League appearances a year later, including the goal that earned City promotion in a 2-2 home draw against Bournemouth.

He resumed the new season in the Third Division as striking partner to Bernie Wright, who had joined the club from Walsall midway through the previous campaign to help City's promotion drive and played 38 matches – 10 of them as substitute – as the side struggled and were ultimately relegated.

Cooke also struggled to hold his place as first-choice striker after David McNiven joined the club from Leeds United, and, although he played 16 matches as partner to McNiven, the following season he left in the January to join Peterborough in a £45,000 deal that brought midfield player Lammie Robertson to Valley Parade. However, he stayed only eight months at Peterborough before he was on the move again – this time to Oxford for £40,000, and in two seasons there he made 72 League appearances, scoring 13 goals. His next move was to Exeter in June 1981 in a £25,000 deal.

Roy McFarland brought him back to Valley Parade in 1982, initially on a month's loan and then permanently in a £10,000 deal, to strengthen his promotion-seeking squad. Cooke played 22 matches to the end of the season as central-defensive partner to McFarland and Jackson as City secured the second promotion place. He made 34 League appearances the following season, but he lost his central-defensive role when former England defender Trevor Cherry replaced McFarland as player-manager.

Injuries restricted Cooke's appearances in what turned out to be his final season at Valley Parade as Cherry and Jackson became the first-choice central-defenders, and he moved to Rochdale in June 1984 after being given a free transfer by City. He became captain during his two years at Rochdale, where he made 75 League appearances before signing for Wrexham for £8,000. He played 51 League matches at Wrexham, where he was also captain, and retired with an impressive 564 League appearances to his name – 600-plus if Cup matches are taken into account.

Cooke, who runs fitness clubs in Cleckheaton and Leeds with his wife Kath, said 'It was nice to finish my career on a high, playing in the European Cup-winners' Cup with Wrexham after we had qualified by winning the Welsh Cup the previous season, but they have changed the rules now and Welsh clubs who play in the English League don't qualify any more. It was a great experience.

'I had a couple of promotions with City, and I enjoyed playing alongside Roy McFarland. It was a great learning experience even at that time of my career, and it was just a pity he left the club the season after we gained promotion. I enjoyed my career, but the players have a different lifestyle nowadays. We were doing well in my day as regards income compared with the man in the street, but there was not nearly as big a gap as there is nowadays.'

Ian Cooper

Date of birth: 21 September 1946

Bradford City record:
Appearances: League 443, FA Cup 29, League Cup 21
Goals: League 4, League Cup 1
Debut: 21 August 1965 v Torquay United

Also played for: Guiseley

Only Ces Podd has played more matches for City than Ian Cooper, who was a consistent defender for his home-town club for 12 seasons between 1965 and 1977. He captained a Bradford Boys side that included future City players Bruce Bannister, Phil Barlow and Steve Ingle and also played alongside Bannister for Yorkshire Schoolboys before joining City in September 1962. He made his debut while still an amateur, before becoming a full-time professional soon afterwards – in August 1966 – after giving up a PE course at Leeds Carnegie College. He was the quiet man of the team, but behind that unassuming character was a steely determination, and he never gave less than his best at the heart of the City defence as he played in 443 League matches and 50 Cup games.

Such was his consistency that Cooper was an ever present in four seasons – 1967–68, 1970–71, 1971–72 and 1972–73 – as he savoured the ups and downs of Bradford City life and held the club's appearance record until it was broken by teammate Ces Podd. He was appointed club captain in 1972–73 and made 154 consecutive League appearances between August 1970 and November 1973.

During his 12 years at Valley Parade, Cooper suffered disappointment as City had to apply for re-election for the third time in their history in 1966, after making his debut in a home match against Torquay at the start of the season. Then, after another disappointment – missing out on promotion by one place in 1968 – he shared the delight of winning promotion the following season but suffered relegation three years later.

City regained their Third Division status in 1976–77, but Cooper made only five appearances in what proved to be his last season. He was given a free transfer at the end of the season and a testimonial. Former teammate Graham Oates brought a Newcastle United team to Valley Parade for the match. Unfortunately, a crowd of only 3,292 turned up for the match, which was a disappointing end to his City career. After leaving Valley Parade he played non-League football for three years with Guiseley.

Cooper said of his time in the game 'I thoroughly enjoyed my football career. It was a great time – what else could you want – being paid to keep fit. In those days the players tended to live locally so we socialised together and went out together at least once a month.

'I have lots of good memories, among them beating Norwich 2–1 in the FA Cup fifth round at Carrow Road. I remember sitting in the dressing room after the match and there was a feeling of sheer elation. We were never expected to win. Sometimes things go right for you, and we took advantage that night. That win set up a quarter-final match against Southampton at Valley Parade. We lost 1–0, but I thought we deserved a replay. We had the chances, but they just wouldn't go in. We had a bit of luck at Norwich, but we didn't have any against Southampton, who went on to win the Cup.

'Another Cup match I remember was our third-round tie against Tottenham Hotspur at Valley Parade in 1990, when we came back from 2–0 down to draw 2–2.

'I played alongside some good players, especially the Welsh international Ken Leek. In those days the ball was heavy and you had to strike it well to get anywhere, and I always remember how he used to pass the ball across the field from left midfield to John Hall on the right wing. That was a great strike in those days because the balls were so heavy.

'I also enjoyed playing down the left side with winger Don Hutchins – I think we played well together. Gerry Ingram had a fantastic workrate, Rod Johnson was a good player and Tom Hallett was a good man to have around.'

Terry Dolan

Date of birth: 11 June 1950

Bradford City record:
Appearances: League 195, FA Cup 9, League Cup 13
Goals: League 43, FA Cup 3, League Cup 3
Debut: 25 August 1976 v Swansea City

Also played for: Bradford Park Avenue, Huddersfield Town, Rochdale
Managed: Bradford City, Rochdale, Hull City, York City, Guiseley

Bradford-born Terry Dolan made a huge contribution to football in his home city, both on and off the field, during a 20-year spell. In that time he played for both City and Park Avenue as well as coaching and managing City, taking them to the verge of the old First Division, only to lose in the Second Division Play-offs.

Dolan had been a City supporter since he was three years old but was rejected by the club as a youngster and joined Park Avenue in 1969, after his father had arranged a trial. He played 48 League matches in Park Avenue's last two seasons as a League club, and when they were voted out of the League in May 1970 a big chance presented itself. 'That pre-season I went to Arsenal for a trial, but I just couldn't live in London, and that is my only regret because the following season Arsenal did the double under manager Bertie Mee, and I could have easily been in that first-team squad.'

So, he resumed the new season with Park Avenue in the Northern Premier League, but he said 'Fortunately, three months later, I moved to Huddersfield Town, which meant I could live at home. They had just been promoted to the old First Division and stayed there for two seasons, which meant I played on all the big grounds in the country.'

Unfortunately, Huddersfield were relegated in 1972 and continued falling as they dropped into the old Fourth Division in five seasons. Dolan, who was captain for two seasons, said 'My biggest disappointment was that once we were relegated a lot of the best players like Trevor Cherry, Roy Ellam and Frank Worthington left and manager Ian Greaves moved to Bolton.'

Dolan joined City in August 1976 for £10,000 after turning down Barnsley, and in his first season the Bantams gained promotion from the old Fourth Division under Bobby Kennedy, but they were relegated the following season. They had a great chance to go back up in 1979-80 under George Mulhall, but missed out on fourth place after losing at Peterborough in the last match of the season, while four other results went against them, but Dolan was on the bench for that vital game and only played for the last 15 minutes.

'I enjoyed my time as a player at Valley Parade,' he said. 'For the first four seasons I didn't miss many games, and I scored my fair share of goals, but then George Mulhall wanted me to play wide right in a 4-4-2 formation, which I didn't enjoy – I saw myself as more of a centre-back or midfield player.'

Mulhall left towards the end of the following season, and Dolan said 'Although I had another year of contract left, I wasn't a regular in the side and our new manager Roy McFarland said "I don't want you to go, but I don't want to stand in your way."' He moved to Rochdale and played there for two years but was released at the end of his contract and went into coaching, while also playing non-League football at Thackley and Harrogate Town.

Dolan then got a job with Bradford Council helping to set up their Football Development Scheme, and that provided a way back to Valley Parade. City used to train on the artificial pitch at the council-owned Scholemoor Sports Centre where Dolan was assistant manager. The YTS scheme had started, and manager Trevor Cherry offered him the job as full-time youth coach in February 1985, during the Third Division Championship, three months before the Valley Parade fire. In the summer of 1986 assistant manager Terry Yorath moved to Swansea, and Cherry promoted Dolan to take his place.

Six months later Cherry himself was sacked, and after a spell as caretaker manager Dolan was appointed manager. 'I had two great years in charge,' he said. 'Supporters will remember those two seasons as an exciting time. My priority was a good team spirit because that is worth a good few points every season. I took over when we were bottom of the table, and we altered the system, started playing with a sweeper and the transformation over the following season was incredible. It was the only time as a manager that I had money to spend, and we bought Paul Tomlinson, Lee Sinnott and Brian Mitchell, and brought in Ron Futcher on transfer deadline day in my first season.'

City had a great chance of promotion at the end of Dolan's second season, but missed out on an automatic promotion place before losing in the Play-offs. He said 'Unfortunately, we lost to Ipswich in the last match, but had we drawn we would have been promoted automatically because of the way the other results went, and then we lost to Middlesbrough in the Play-offs after extra-time in the second leg. The damage was done when we couldn't strengthen the squad – we had Andy Townsend and Keith Curle lined up. I felt it was time to speculate, but the board didn't agree. We only had a squad of 14 or 15, and against Ipswich we had John Hendrie suspended and Greg Abbott was carried off. If we had had one or two extra players we would have got away with anything.'

Dolan recovered from his sacking at Valley Parade by embarking on a long managerial career at Rochdale, Hull City and York City. Then in the autumn of 2006 he returned to management at non-League Guiseley.

Peter Downsborough

Date of birth: 13 September 1943

Bradford City record:
Appearances: League 225, FA Cup 14, League Cup 13
Debut: 22 December 1973 v Crewe Alexandra

Also played for: Halifax Town, Swindon Town

Bradford City have had few better goalkeepers than Peter Downsborough, who made 252 League and Cup appearances over six seasons before he retired in 1980. He wasn't particularly tall for a goalkeeper and did not command the area, but he had few equals as a shot stopper. Although he played 252 League and Cup matches for City, including 225 in the League, it's true to say that Downsborough's best spell was his eight years at Swindon where he won a League Cup-winners' medal after the Third Division club's sensational 3-1 win over Arsenal in the 1969 Final.

Halifax-born Downsborough was an all-round sportsman at school, playing football, Rugby Union, cricket and winning honours at swimming and boxing, but he chose football for a living and was signed by his home-town club in 1960 by accident. He had been selected as centre-forward for a Halifax Boys match against Rotherham Boys but went in goal following an injury to the regular goalkeeper, and he played so well that he caught the eye of Halifax Town scouts and signed for them.

He made his League debut for the Shaymen against Bournemouth in 1960 and turned full-time professional the following season. Downsborough played 148 League matches in four years for the club, but it wasn't a happy period for them. They were relegated to the Fourth Division in 1963 and had to apply for re-election in 1965.

Downsborough moved to Swindon that year in an exchange deal which involved forward Bill Atkins joining Halifax and a £3,000 cash adjustment. It proved to be a great move for Downsborough, who found himself in a fine Swindon team, which featured defender John Trollope, who played 767 League matches in a 20-year career at the County Ground, along with winger Don Rogers, who played 400 League matches for them and was one of the stars of the League Cup Final triumph.

As well as helping Swindon to win the League Cup, Downsborough also helped them to gain promotion into the Second Division, as well as winning an Anglo-Italian Cup-winners' medal against AS Roma. He made 274 League appearances – and three on loan with Brighton – before returning to West Yorkshire to sign for City in November 1973. Initially he came on loan, but the transfer was made permanent two months later when City paid Swindon a £5,000 fee.

City had been relegated to the Fourth Division two seasons earlier, and the only success Downsborough enjoyed during his spell at Valley Parade was helping the club to reach the FA Cup quarter-final for the first time in 56 years in 1975–76 – they lost 1–0 to the eventual Cup winners Southampton at Valley Parade – and promotion to the Third Division the following season. Unfortunately, they were relegated back to the 'Fourth' after just one season.

Amid all these largely barren years, Downsborough's performances shone like a beacon. Week after week, this unassuming player produced top-class displays, and such was his consistency that he was an ever present in 1974–75 and the relegation season in 1977–78, while he missed only one match the season before when City won promotion.

If any player deserved a successful testimonial it was Peter Downsborough. Unfortunately, only 1,026 attended his testimonial match against Huddersfield Town in May 1980 – the year he announced his retirement. Sadly, he was not fit enough to play, and I have vivid memories of the sad sight of him limping around Valley Parade on crutches signing autographs for the few people who turned up to say farewell to him.

Donald Duckett

Date of birth: 1894

Bradford City record:
Appearances: League 155, FA Cup 10
Goals: League 6, FA Cup 1
Debut: 8 September 1919 v Burnley

Also played for: Bradford Park Avenue, Halifax Town

For services to West Yorkshire football, Donald Duckett would take some beating. The Bradford-born half-back – born in the Thornton district of the city – played the whole of his 15-year career at three clubs – City, Halifax Town and Bradford Park Avenue.

Duckett joined City from a junior club at Queensbury in April 1914 as a 20-year-old – four months before World War One broke out. Although the war delayed his start in League football, he established himself in wartime football and topped City's wartime appearances, playing in 123 matches in four seasons and scoring 20 goals. So, by the time the League resumed in 1919 he was a regular in the City team and quickly became part of the famous Hargreaves-Storer-Duckett half-back line. Incidentally, Duckett's wage during the season in 1919 was £6 a week. A short, stocky player, he was described by contemporaries as 'a human dynamo of energy, whose skill was on a par with his industry'.

Duckett, who also played at inside-forward, established himself as left-half in City's last three seasons in the First Division and was an ever present with 42 appearances in City's relegation season in 1921-22. He continued to play for City in the Second Division, but he made only three appearances in what turned out to be his final season and was transferred to Halifax Town midway through the campaign in December 1924.

Apparently, City felt that at 30 Duckett was past his best, but after recovering from injury he set out to prove them wrong. He spent almost three years at Halifax in the Third Division North before he returned to Bradford to play with Park Avenue in November 1927. He signed for Avenue while he was in bed under observation for smallpox, and, by coincidence, his first match was against City. By that time Avenue had dropped into the Third Division North, but he helped them to win promotion in his first season and was made captain after they were promoted, before being forced to retire with knee trouble in March 1929.

Writing in the *Yorkshire Sports* 25 years later, Duckett said 'The most thrilling match of my career was when I made my first appearance with Avenue, for it happened to be against City, my old club, and Tommy Cairns was up against me. I was brought into a winning team, and I knew the directors would be condemned for changing it if things went wrong, but we won 5-0 so it was a happy day for me.

'The biggest moment of my career in Bradford came when I was appointed captain of Avenue after we had won promotion. I always think I played my better football with Avenue than ever I had done with City – and that after they discarded me at Valley Parade because they thought I was near the end of my tether.

'My unhappiest moment was when I was in the Avenue team beaten 6-0 at West Bromwich Albion. I had been in and out of St Luke's Hospital for knee treatment and that Cup tie was the last match I ever played in any sort of football. I was medically advised to give up the game, which I did, but it was a wrench.'

Duckett, whose uncle Horace was capped twice for England at Rugby Union, became a successful businessman in Bradford when he retired from football.

Lee Duxbury

Date of birth: 7 October 1969

Bradford City record:
Appearances: League 272, FA Cup 16, League Cup 21
Goals: League 32, League Cup 3
Debut: 13 May 1989 v Manchester City

Also played for: Rochdale (loan), Huddersfield Town, Oldham Athletic, Bury

Bradford City may have had more skilful players, but few worked as hard at their game as Lee Duxbury. He was an industrious midfield player, who would tackle, pass and run all through the game, setting an example to those around him, so it was no surprise that he was captain with his two principal clubs, City and Oldham Athletic.

Duxbury, who is now happily part of the coaching staff at Oldham, can look back with pride on a 15-year career that saw him make 595 League appearances, scoring 66 goals, which included two winning Wembley appearances in the Play-offs with Huddersfield Town and Bradford City. The bulk of his appearances were with those clubs – 272 in two spells at Valley Parade and 222 with Oldham.

The Keighley-born player joined City as a schoolboy and worked his way up from there to become first-team captain, making 209 League appearances before he left the club for the first time in December 1994 to join Huddersfield in a part exchange deal, which meant he and Lee Sinnott joined Town, while defender Graham Mitchell came to Valley Parade.

After helping Huddersfield to promotion through the Play-offs in 1995, he returned to City to help in their Play-off success the following year before leaving Valley Parade for a second time, joining Oldham in a £350,000 deal. After seven years at Boundary Park, he had a season at Bury before calling time on his League career.

Duxbury recalls 'I signed for City as a schoolboy and became full-time the year after the fire. In fact, our young goalkeeper Mark Evans and I were in the section of the stand where the fire started, and we left the stand five minutes before half-time to go for a drink. By the time we had walked 50 yards the flames were above us, but luckily we got on to the pitch.

'I got a couple of first-team appearances in 1988–89 when I came off the bench against West Ham and at home to Manchester City in the last match of the season. I then went on loan to Rochdale for three months, and I came back a different player, going into the first team and becoming captain. In fact, I captained the team at Hull at the end of the 1989–90 season when we lost 2–1 – a result that sent us down.

'I was a first-team regular for the next four and a half seasons before the club sold Lee Sinnott and I to Huddersfield Town just before Christmas in 1994, with Graham Mitchell coming to Bradford in part exchange.

'I played for Huddersfield when we gained promotion through the Play-offs, which was good, but I got injured at the start of the following season, and after I recovered they decided to sell me back to City. I also went to the Play-off Final with Bradford in May 1996 and we also won against Notts County.

'So, I was on the winning side at Wembley twice in successive seasons, but I enjoyed it better the second time around because I knew what to expect. The first time everything flashed past me.

'The following February I was on the move again. Chris Kamara told me the club had had a bid from Oldham for £350,000 and the chairman, Geoffrey Richmond, had accepted it. I couldn't believe they had done that – they were getting rid of me – and people talk about loyalty.

'The deal was done, but then Oldham beat Queen's Park Rangers on the Saturday and we lost to Manchester City at home, and suddenly the deal was off because Chris Kamara turned round and said to me "If you go to Oldham and Oldham stay up it won't look right for me."

'So, I said to him "You give me the new contract that Oldham were giving me" – but the chairman said no. It wasn't good man management. The deal was eventually sorted, but it left a bitter taste in my mouth because I thought I was going to be at Bradford City for the rest of my career. I felt comfortable at the club and to sell me a year and a half after rejoining them was disappointing because I thought I was playing well, but you go where you are wanted.

'Oldham obviously offered me a lot more money, and when Bradford refused to let me go I asked them for the same amount. I spent seven happy years at Oldham; I was made captain straightaway and remained captain until I left in 2003, and I took all my coaching badges there.

'I then spent a year at Bury before my body told me that enough was enough. I had played some 700 League and Cup matches and it wasn't as if I was a centre-half or right-back – I was a box to box midfield player.'

Duxbury spent a year at Farsley Celtic where his old City and Huddersfield teammate Lee Sinnott was manager and also played in Northern Ireland in the 2005–06 season. 'I had a mate who is assistant manager at Glenavon, and from Christmas onwards I flew to Northern Ireland on Fridays to play there – it was good experience,' he said.

'I wanted to be a player-manager, but then my Oldham teammate, now manager, John Sheridan offered me the job at Oldham, and I am also working with my Oldham and Bradford teammate Tommy Wright who is assistant manager. I am training and doing some coaching. My official job is reserve-team manager, but we share out the training.'

Roy Ellam

Date of birth: 13 January 1943

Bradford City record:
Appearances: League 149, FA Cup 6, League Cup 7
Goals: League 12, FA Cup 1
Debut: 7 October 1961 v Gillingham

Also played for: Huddersfield Town, Leeds United, Philadelphia Atoms, Washington Diplomats, Mossley, Gainsborough Trinity
Managed: Gainsborough Trinity

Roy Ellam developed into a reliable and versatile defender, happy at full-back or in the centre of the defence, after joining Bradford City as a 16-year-old in 1959. Born at Hemsworth in South Yorkshire, Ellam attracted scouts while playing for South Elmsall Boys and was offered the chance to join Queen's Park Rangers before deciding to sign for City, first as an amateur and then as full-time professional in April 1960.

He had to wait two years for his League debut, which came when he was 18 in a 3-1 defeat at Gillingham in October 1961 – the season after City had been relegated to the Fourth Division. He played at left-back that day and four days later he made his home debut against Southport. His full-back partner that night was fellow 18-year-old player Brian Kelly, and they set a record for the youngest full-back pairing in the club's history – an aggregate total of 37 years and 48 days.

Ellam appeared in five consecutive matches before dropping out of the side for the rest of the campaign. However, he achieved a regular place the following season, first as a deputy for Mike Smith in the middle of the defence before settling in at left-back when Smith returned to the side. However, it was a miserable season for the club as they were forced to seek re-election for the second time in their history.

There were changes the following season after the retirement of captain Tom Flockett. Kelly took over at right-back from Flockett, while Ellam replaced Stan Storton at left-back. The new pair of full-backs were ever presents in 1963-64, along with goalkeeper Bernard Fisher, as City agonisingly missed out on promotion by one place after losing their last two matches, including the crucial final home game against promotion rivals Workington.

There were more changes the following season as manager Bob Brocklebank was replaced by former Welsh international Harris, and City struggled to avoid having to apply for re-election. Ellam began the season as partner to Kelly, but Kelly left to join Doncaster Rovers after losing his place to Bradford-born teenager Steve Ingle, and although Ellam played at left-back for most of the campaign, he also played at left-half and centre in the last two months of the season, proving his versatility.

City narrowly avoided having to apply for re-election, but that proved to be his last full season at Valley Parade. He was always likely to move to a higher grade of football, and he got his chance in January 1966. City were looking to solve their goalscoring problems and decided to exchange Ellam for Derek Stokes, who had been a huge success at Valley Parade before joining Huddersfield Town nearly six years earlier.

Unfortunately for City, Stokes failed to reproduce the goalscoring form of his first spell, but Ellam proved to be a big success at Huddersfield, and when Town won the old Second Division Championship in 1969-70, he was one of seven ever presents, and he made 206 League appearances in six and a half years there.

Some key players left Huddersfield following their relegation, among them future City manager Trevor Cherry, who was transferred to Leeds United, and Ellam followed him to Elland Road two months later. However, while Cherry was a success at Leeds, playing more than 400 League and Cup matches during a 10-year career there, Ellam struggled to break into Don Revie's team. United were not only one of the top three teams in England, but one of the best in Europe, containing the likes of Billy Bremner, Johnny Giles, Norman Hunter, Jack Charlton, Paul Madeley, Eddie Gray and other internationals, and the gap was too big for Ellam to bridge. So, he made only 11 League appearances in two seasons at Elland Road before returning to Huddersfield, who, by this time, were on the slide down the divisions.

He made only 18 League appearances in his second spell at Leeds Road before trying his luck in the US, where he played with Philadelphia Atoms and Washington Diplomats in the NASL and then continued his career with non-League Mossley and Gainsborough Trinity, where he was also manager.

Mark Ellis

Date of birth: 6 January 1962

Bradford City record:
Appearances: League 218, FA Cup 18, League Cup 23
Goals: League 30, FA Cup 2, League Cup 1
Debut: 11 April 1981 v Wigan Athletic

Also played for: Halifax Town

Bradford-born Mark Ellis made 218 League appearances, mainly as a left-winger, during the 1980s until a knee injury curtailed his career.

Ellis was playing local football at 15 when City – then managed by George Mulhall – invited him for a trial, and he recalls 'I trained at night while playing for the juniors on Saturday mornings. I also played for the reserves for the first time when I was 16. Then, when I was 17, I was invited to play for Leeds United juniors against Doncaster Rovers and came on as a substitute.'

The Leeds interest spurred City into action, and immediately afterwards they signed Ellis as a non-contract player. Ellis made his debut after coming on as substitute in a 3–3 draw at home to Wigan Athletic in April 1981 and his full debut in a 2–0 defeat at Doncaster Rovers a fortnight later. The popular winger, nicknamed 'Megga' by his teammates, made 16 League appearances as City gained promotion to the Third Division under player-manager Roy McFarland the following season, and he has special memories of that season, not least the third-round League Cup tie against Ipswich, then a leading First Division club managed by Bobby Robson. City drew 1–1 at Portman Road but lost the replay 3–2 after extra-time.

Ellis made 25 League appearances the following season, as player-manager Trevor Cherry began to put his Third Division Championship team together, and recalls missing only one match in the title season itself – the match at Bolton on May Day Bank Holiday Monday when City won 2–0 to make sure of the Championship – before returning for the last match against Lincoln City and the horrors of the fire disaster.

He struggled for a regular place in the Second Division side the following season, after Cherry signed his former Leeds United teammate and Scottish international Arthur Graham, making only 13 League appearances plus 12 as substitute, but he played in 31 League matches the following season as Graham faded out of the first-team picture to become youth-team coach when Terry Dolan succeeded Cherry as manager.

The following season began well for Ellis, as City mounted a realistic promotion challenge, but it all went wrong for him at Birmingham City on Saturday 5 March when he went off with a knee injury, which meant he missed the heartache of losing to Middlesbrough in the Play-offs.

He recalls 'I had a cartilage operation, but then the surgeon told me there was cruciate ligament damage, and I had a massive operation. That is the worst thing that can happen to any footballer. Even after this second operation I struggled. Knowing what I know now, I wouldn't have had a cruciate ligament operation done. I was out of action for a year.'

Sadly, Ellis made only 11 more League appearances for City, four of them as a substitute, after that injury at Birmingham, but he particularly remembers scoring in the 1–1 home draw against Manchester City in the last match of the 1988–89 season.

He left Valley Parade at 28, having made 218 League appearances, including 28 as substitute, and scoring 30 goals. Ellis finished his career at Halifax Town, making 37 League appearances and scoring four goals, but admits 'I didn't enjoy it there, and I went to play at Cape Town.'

The move to South Africa proved to be productive for him because he got the chance to work with the academy run by the top Dutch team Ajax. 'I learned so much from the Dutch guys. I started coaching when I finished playing and gradually built up my qualifications,' he said.

Now Ellis is busy coaching not only in England but also in the US. He coaches at Thomas Danby College in Leeds and runs an under-19s team in the English Colleges League and also works for the Huddersfield Town Academy running the under-14s team, although he stresses 'my loyalties lie at Bradford City.' Then in 2006 he took on another job, becoming assistant manager to former City teammate Terry Dolan at Guiseley.

He began his own coaching agency in Detroit, Michigan, six years ago, running the scheme for two months in the summer while the rest of the year is spent recruiting people to go on the scheme. He also recruits for the university, helping to give footballers a free education through football depending on how good they are academically and how good their skills are. 'It is like a second chance for good footballers to go to America for coaching and get a degree as well.'

Ellis is also involved in a new senior club in Detroit – two divisions below the major Leagues – and helps to coach the players. He is optimistic for the future of the new club. 'There is space to establish a major League soccer team there,' he said. 'Soccer is massive at youth level in the USA and there are lots of opportunities in sport and a lot of money available for football and education. There are so many opportunities in coaching now. I really enjoy it – I am lucky to be involved in football.'

Dave Evans

Date of birth: 20 May 1958

Bradford City record:
Appearances: League 223, FA Cup 14, League Cup 23
Goals: League 3, FA Cup 1
Debut: 25 August 1984 v Cambridge United

Also played for: Aston Villa, Halifax Town

Player-manager Trevor Cherry made two crucial signings as he put together his team to make a realistic promotion challenge in the summer of 1984. One of them was Coventry winger John Hendrie, the other was Halifax Town defender Dave Evans – then 26 – both on free transfers, and what superb signings they turned out to be as City won the Third Division Championship in their first season. For Hendrie was an ever present and Evans missed only one match and was voted player of the year by one of the supporters' organisations.

Cherry and his assistant Terry Yorath wanted a defender who was comfortable on the ball and could play it constructively out of defence. Evans fitted that bill perfectly, and he gave City fine service for six seasons, making 223 League appearances.

However, Evans almost joined local rivals Huddersfield Town when he was leaving Halifax. 'My contract was up at the Shay, and I was on a week to week basis. The only way to tempt me to stay would be for them to offer me more money, but they couldn't do that so I left on a free transfer. John McGrath at Mansfield was interested in me, along with Mick Buxton at Huddersfield. I spoke to Mick Buxton and told him 'I will probably sign tomorrow.' But that night the Bradford chairman Stafford Heginbotham phoned me and offered me more money and that changed my mind. Joining City was the best decision I ever made. My time at Bradford City was the best and most enjoyable in my career.'

West Bromwich-born Evans began his career as an apprentice with Aston Villa and made his debut at right-back against Barcelona in a UEFA Cup quarter-final against Barcelona at Villa Park. However, he made only two League appearances in the First Division with Villa before moving on loan to Halifax in September 1978 before they signed him the following summer for a club record £22,500 when George Kirby was manager at the Shay. He made 218 League appearances in six years there but admits 'It went stale' and moved to City.

Evans began his Valley Parade career as central-defensive partner to Peter Jackson, who captained the 1984–85 Third Division Championship team, and that partnership continued for most of the following season as City established themselves in the Second Division, despite not being able to play at their own ground after Valley Parade was wrecked by the fire, but when Terry Dolan succeeded Cherry as manager he gave Evans the key role as sweeper, playing behind central-defenders Lee Sinnott and Gavin Oliver.

He was an ever present in 1986–87 as City finished 10th and missed only one match the following season in the failed promotion bid. Evans enjoyed playing as sweeper.

'The whole thing fell apart when John Docherty was brought in to replace Terry Yorath,' said Evans. 'Docherty didn't endear himself to people in the club and rubbed a lot of people up the wrong way. In fact, the players didn't like him at all. It had always been a family club, and we were all together as a club, players and supporters, and we seemed to lose that when John Docherty arrived. The football he wanted us to play was awful. He didn't seem to have any idea of the way he wanted to play, unlike our previous managers Trevor Cherry, Terry Yorath, Terry Dolan and Stan Ternent. I had another 12 months left on my contract and Docherty told me I could leave on a free transfer if I wanted to, so I re-joined Halifax.

'We had some good players at that time and played some attractive football, with the likes of Chris Lucketti and Paul Futcher in the team, but all of a sudden it went downhill. In the last season I was there I wasn't playing as often as I would like. Halifax offered me the job of youth-team manager, and I went to the USA to do some coaching and think about the offer, but then I had a call from my wife Jane to say she had read the club were scrapping the youth system.'

So, Evans retired from football, having made 516 League appearances, including 73 League matches in his second spell at Halifax. 'After I left the game in 1992 I trained to be a policeman and passed my examinations and was about to join the West Yorkshire police force when the Government decided to close down recruitment. So, I joined Pearl Assurance as a financial adviser, and I work for the PFA as a financial adviser, which involves advising players about their pensions. I also did some scouting for Huddersfield when Peter Jackson was there the first time and coached at their Academy, but I don't enjoy watching football now. It is too clinical and any physical contact has been taken out of the game. I enjoy Rugby Union and Rugby League because those games are still physical. Nowadays, footballers are athletes who play football, whereas they used to be footballers who were athletes.'

Jock Ewart

Date of birth: 1891
Died: 1943

Bradford City record:
Appearances: League 283, FA Cup 19
Goals: None
Debut: 7 September 1912 v Aston Villa

Also played for: Bellshill Rovers, Bellshill Athletic, Larkhall Thistle, Airdrieonians, Preston North End

Jock Ewart was not only a popular goalkeeper but one of City's best in a Valley Parade career that spanned 14 years. The Scottish international, who joined City in May 1912 – a year after they had won the FA Cup – totalled 283 League appearances – 214 of them in the First Division – and eventually replaced Cup Final hero Mark Mellors.

Ewart delighted supporters with his agility, positional sense and, occasionally, his antics. He was particularly adept at saving penalties, taking delight in trying to put off the penalty taker by moving along the line, not to mention saying a few choice words to the player concerned.

In fact, it was partly through his antics – and the antics of other goalkeepers – that the penalty law was changed during the 1920s, which forced goalkeepers not to move until the ball had been kicked.

Teammate Dickie Bond wrote, many years later, of Ewart's tactics. He told the *Yorkshire Sports* 'He would come out to the spot and move the ball off it and ask who was taking the penalty, though he generally knew. Then he would turn to the kicker and politely say "Ye takkin' a penalty mon? Hoots, ye couldna' hit the stand!" It was all done with the idea of putting the taker off his stride and rattling him, and how well it worked out. I always say Jock saved many penalties for us with his tongue as well as with his hands.'

Ewart first played football with Douglas Park, a junior club near his home at Oakbank, before moving to Bellshill Rovers, Bellshill Athletic and Larkhall Thistle. He signed as a professional with Airdrieonians in March 1909 and quickly gained representative honours, playing for the Scottish League against the Irish League in 1910 and the Southern League in 1911.

City signed him for £1,200, and during his long Valley Parade career Ewart wrote for himself a special place in the club's history. He made his debut in the first match of the 1912-13 season at home to Aston Villa and played in 33 out of 38 matches in that first campaign, 32 in the second season, while he missed only one match in 1914-15 when football continued despite World War One.

Ewart resumed his career after the war, despite suffering shell shock while on active service, and in 1921 he achieved every Scottish player's ambition when he played for Scotland against England and helped them to a 3-0 win in Glasgow. It was his only Scottish cap, and it came 10 years after his first international trial.

He made 40 appearances, missing only two matches, in the 1919-20 season, 37 the following campaign and 35 in the season City were relegated. After missing only one match the following season – the first back in the Second Division – Airdrieonians persuaded him to rejoin them. They paid £300 for Ewart, and he helped them to a Scottish Cup triumph over Hibernian before he returned to City in May 1927, after his successor Jim McLaren had moved to Leicester City following the club's relegation. He made 28 League appearances in what was City's first season in the Third Division North, but he left at the end of that campaign to join Preston North End, bringing to an end his long association with the club and a proud record of 302 League and Cup appearances spread over eight seasons.

He played for Preston in Alex James's last season and toured North America with them in May 1929, but two years later, four months after he retired, he was suspended sine die by the FA for his alleged involvement in a match-rigging affair surrounding a City match against Bury. He returned to football as a trainer with New Brighton when his suspension was lifted, and he eventually became a publican. He died in Bradford in 1943.

Tom Flockett

Date of birth: 17 July 1927
Died: 1997

Bradford City record:
Appearances: League 227, FA Cup 18, League Cup 5
Goals: League 1
Debut: 24 August 1957 v Stockport County

Also played for: Chesterfield

Bradford City had few more consistent players than Tom Flockett during a successful six-year spell at Valley Parade in the late 1950s and early 1960s. The rugged, no nonsense right-back rarely had a bad game and was liked and respected by teammates and supporters alike.

Those were the days before the overlapping full-back, whose job is not only to defend, but join the attack down the flanks. In Flockett's day, full-backs were defenders, marking their respective wingers and then clearing the danger.

Flockett had few equals in the lower divisions as a right-back in his day, and although he was not particularly blessed with pace, he was good on recovery and a master of the sliding tackle, which he used effectively to stop wingers who were quicker than himself, much to the delight of his army of admirers in the stands and terraces.

Flockett, who was from the North East, was born at Ferryhill and joined Chesterfield from Spennymoor United, signing as a professional in April 1949. He made 200 League appearances in eight years at Saltergate, before joining City in June 1957, succeeding an equally rugged, no nonsense right-back, Jock Whyte, as a new full-back partner to George Mulholland. He was one of manager Peter Jackson's best signings, and such was Flockett's impact at Valley Parade that he was an ever present in his first season, and it was no surprise that he became City captain.

Although injuries restricted him to 22 League matches the following season, he made 40 League appearances in 1959-60 and missed only one of City's seven FA Cup matches as the club reached the fifth round of the competition before being knocked out by Burnley in a replay at Turf Moor. He missed only one match in 1960-61, when City were relegated to the Fourth Division, and played 40 matches the following season when City missed out on promotion by one place.

One of my abiding memories of Flockett came in that 1961-62 campaign, when City played Arsenal at Highbury in a third-round FA Cup tie. There was no danger of an upset as Arsenal won 3-0 and Flockett faced a big test against the Gunners' flying left-winger Alan Skirton. Flockett used his experience to limit the danger posed by Skirton, playing deep to prevent him from being exposed for pace, while the Arsenal man was also

the victim of some of the full-back's sliding tackles.

Flockett made 34 League appearances in what proved to be his final season, but his Valley Parade career ended on a sad note as City were forced to seek re-election for the second time in their history. He left City, having made 227 League appearances and played in 23 Cup games, but he scored only one goal, which showed where his priorities lay.

One of Flockett's many admirers in the Valley Parade dressing room was centre-half Jim Lawlor, who said 'Not only was Tom a good player, but he was a good friend to have around, and we had a good dressing room in those days. He was a smashing bloke and a very dependable right-back. He would never let you down through lack of effort. He was very knowledgeable about the game. He played with a lot of good players at Chesterfield and played against a lot of good players, and he could always advise his teammates against the strengths and weaknesses of opponents.'

After leaving Bradford, Flockett returned to Chesterfield to coach the junior players and later worked in industry in the town, where he died in 1997 aged 70.

Oscar Fox

Date of birth: 1889
Died: 1947

Bradford City record:
Appearances: League 164, FA Cup 11
Goals: League 57, FA Cup 3
Debut: 18 February 1911 v Oldham Athletic

Also played for: Castleford Town

Charlie Fox, front row, second from left, in this Bradford City team photograph from September 1919.

Before football formations were changed forever in England when Alf Ramsey's so-called wingless wonders won the World Cup in 1966, the partnership between the winger and his inside-forward was an important part of any team. And Bradford City have had few better inside-forwards in their history than Oscar Fox, who not only partnered their most famous player, England outside-right Dickie Bond, for eight seasons – all in the top division – either side of World War One, but he was a goalscorer as well and was also leading scorer for three consecutive seasons before the war.

Sheffield-born Fox attracted the attention of City when he was playing for Castleford Town and made his debut in 1910-11, when the club achieved their highest-ever placing – fifth in Division One – as well as winning the FA Cup.

Fox, then 21, didn't figure in any of the Cup matches after joining the club in November 1910, but he played his first League match at Oldham in February 1911 and made two more League appearances away to Bristol City and at home to Notts County in his first season at Valley Parade.

Fox had more opportunities the following season as manager Peter O'Rourke began to ring the changes, making 11 League appearances and scoring three goals before establishing a regular place in the side. For three seasons until League football was suspended because of World War One, he was City's leading scorer with 13 goals in 30 League appearances in 1912-13, nine in 33 in 1913-14 and 17 in 36 in 1914-15.

Fox scored 15 goals in 39 wartime matches before returning to help City in what became a battle to stay in the First Division. He scored eight goals in 29 League appearances in 1919-20 and seven in 21 in 1920-21, but then he lost his place in the side for what proved to be the club's last season at the top for 77 years.

Fox made his only appearance in that 1921-22 campaign – and his last senior appearance in City colours – in a 2-1 defeat by Liverpool in January 1922, after receiving a £540 benefit from the League match against Middlesbrough in the October.

He retired to his home in Sheffield with an impressive record – 57 League goals in 164 appearances – all in the First Division – as well as three in 11 Cup matches. He was employed in a billiards saloon in Sheffield and died in his home city in 1947, aged 54. His son, also named Oscar, played as a winger for Sheffield Wednesday and Mansfield Town between 1946 and 1957.

David Fretwell

Date of birth: 18 February 1952

Bradford City record:
Appearances: League 253, FA Cup 18, League Cup 9
Goals: League 5, League Cup 1
Debut: 27 February 1971 v Halifax Town

Also played for: Wigan Athletic, Northwich Victoria, Salisbury

Consistency was the hallmark of David Fretwell's performances over the six seasons he was first choice at the heart of City's defence. He was not a spectacular player, but he went about his work in a quiet, unassuming, but highly-effective way.

His first-team career began when he made his debut in a home match against Halifax Town in February 1971, but he didn't gain a regular place until two years later, following the club's relegation to the Fourth Division. Such was his consistency from then onwards that he missed only 24 League matches out of a possible 252 in six seasons. His best season was undoubtedly City's promotion campaign in 1976-77 when he was the team's only ever present and his partnership with John Middleton, who missed only five matches, was a big factor in their success under manager Bobby Kennedy. Neither were particularly tall for central-defenders, but there was no doubt as to their effectiveness.

Fretwell also made 36 League appearances the following season when City were relegated after just one season in Division Three, but he left at the end of that campaign to play in the US for California Sunshine. He returned to England in October 1978 to join Wigan Athletic under Ian McNeill in their first season in the League. He made 112 League appearances for Wigan, mainly at right-back, before joining non-League Northwich Victoria in July 1981. Joining Northwich proved to be a great move for Fretwell, who played in successive FA Trophy Finals at Wembley in 1982 and 1983 - once as a winner, the other as a loser. 'Playing at Wembley twice is everyone's dream,' he said.

Fretwell also played non-League football at Mossley before he got promoted with Bradford & Bingley and moved to Salisbury and lived in the Winchester and Eastleigh areas. 'I played with Salisbury, but I broke my leg and arm in a car accident and that finished my career,' he said. He was also assistant manager at Salisbury.

He now lives at Cowthorpe in North Yorkshire, looking after 23 branches as area sales manager and took part in negotiations which led to Bradford & Bingley sponsoring City.

Born at Normanton, Fretwell's first connection with the club came in 1967, when he joined them as a 14-year-old. 'We were not allowed on the pitch and trained under the old stand,' he recalls. He was spotted by City while playing for Normanton British Rail and after training with them as a schoolboy he joined them as an amateur in 1967, but he continued his studies at Bradford University, where he gained a Bachelor of Technology degree before turning professional.

The Valley Parade fire disaster had a deeply felt effect on Fretwell, even though he was not there on that tragic day. 'I was at home on the day of the fire when it came on TV, and I thought of the days when my family used to sit there,' he said. 'A friend of mine, Alan Towers, was on the gate that day. He was counting the cash when he heard this shout "fire," and before he knew it a policeman was yanking people out of the stand. He returned the following day and found the coins had melted in the heat. I have lots of footballing memories and I thought of the times that my family sat in the stand.

'I also remember the times I used to train in the stand and you could see where rubbish had been deposited under the floorboards. It is sad because I have some fantastic memories of City and I spent some fantastic years at Valley Parade. If I could, I would do it all over again.

'I remember getting promoted and we had an FA Cup run. I was on £6 a week when I started and then played for £20 a week – part-time because I was at university. When I received my first bonus I got £38, which was a lot of money in those days – the system was a basic wage plus bonuses.

'I am also a Leeds United fan and their results and City's results are the two clubs I look for on Saturdays.'

Allan Gilliver

Date of birth: 3 August 1944

Bradford City record:
Appearances: League 72, FA Cup 6, League Cup 4
Goals: League 30, FA Cup 2
Debut: 12 August 1972 v Barnsley

Also played for: Huddersfield Town, Blackburn Rovers, Rotherham United, Brighton & Hove Albion, Lincoln City, Stockport County, Boston United

Allan Gilliver prides himself on doing every job at Valley Parade except director or team manager during an association with the club going back some 35 years.

A strong, bustling centre-forward, Gilliver scored 32 League and Cup goals in 82 matches in the 1970s, but that does not begin to tell the story of his involvement with Bradford City, which ended with his retirement in April 2007.

His first connection with the club began in the 1972 close season when he joined City from Lincoln. He spent two seasons at Valley Parade and was top scorer in his first season with 19 League goals. He left City two years later to join Stockport, but returned to make two appearances, one as substitute, in the 1978–79 season when his friend George Mulhall had taken over as manager before coming back a second time in 1983 to fulfil a variety of off-the-field roles.

Gilliver began his career at Huddersfield Town in 1961, and after scoring 22 goals in 45 League matches he attracted the attention of Blackburn Rovers, who signed him for £30,000, but they had to repay £18,000 of that fee because of the player's back problems.

He said 'I got the back injury playing for Huddersfield – the disc had collapsed so I had to have it taken out. The back injury stopped me from being the player that everyone thought I was going to be because I lost a yard of pace, and I never had that sharpness in the penalty box that I had before.

'I was out for a year with back trouble and I was the first footballer to have part of his fee returned to the selling club. Rules have changed in football since then that puts the onus on buying clubs to give medicals. In fact, all clubs give medicals nowadays.'

Gilliver scored nine goals in 34 League matches and has no doubt that, of his seven League clubs, Blackburn were 'the best team I played with'. He said 'We had so many internationals in the team like Ronnie Clayton, who captained England, Keith Newton, Bryan Douglas, John Connelly, Barry Hole, Mike England, Andy McEvoy and Adam Blacklaw, but the best full-back I played with was Ray Wilson at Huddersfield – he went on to win the World Cup with England in 1966.'

After leaving Blackburn in 1968, Gilliver moved to Rotherham before being transferred after one season to Brighton, where he stayed for almost two years, scoring 19 goals in 57 League matches. From there he moved to Lincoln for just over a year before City signed him.

He then had a season at Stockport before, at 30, he moved to the US, where efforts were being made to promote the game with money and big-name players like Brazilian legend Pelé at New York Cosmos. Gilliver signed for Baltimore Comets, but a shoulder injury prevented him playing more than a handful of matches.

He returned to England to do some coaching while playing non-League football with Boston United and also helped to coach young players at Valley Parade.

Gilliver, who was also an accomplished cricketer, played for Sussex second team while he was at Brighton. He also played for many years in the Bradford League, achieving the coveted landmark of 1,000 runs in a season while he was at Brighouse. He is also a keen golfer.

He returned to Valley Parade in 1983 to run the bars and was running them on the day of the fire disaster. Gilliver said 'I have done every job except team manager. These jobs include groundsman and stadium manager, which is a big job nowadays following all the safety and crowd control regulations that have come into force in the last 20 years.

'Former chairman Geoffrey Richmond asked me to do the commercial manager's job because I had so many contacts, but it was too much to do that and the stadium manager's job as well, and it put me in hospital with stress. So, I gave up the commercial job and became stadium manager again, as well as helping out with ground maintenance. I have also done the safety officer's job.

'Following the Popplewell Report into the Valley Parade fire and the Taylor Report into the Hillsborough disaster, we have super stadia and everything has got to be checked every year. We also have to employ 100 stewards for every match, which is expensive for clubs and costs us about £3,000 a match.

'I have seen the ups and downs of the club, including administration and receivership crises and changes in the game itself. Football is played at a fast pace nowadays, but what makes a good game of football is the crowd. Crowds in our day were a lot bigger, but nowadays there are so many other things to do and it is very expensive going to football now.'

David Gray

Date of birth: 13 April 1923

Bradford City record:
Appearances: League 242, FA Cup 15
Goals: League 13
Debut: 11 September 1948 v Stockport County

Also played for: Ossett Town

For six seasons in the 1950s versatile David Gray was a regular and consistent player in a variety of positions in Bradford City's Third Division North side. He was regarded mainly as a strong tackling right-half, but he played in both inside-forward positions as well as right-back and left-half in nine years at Valley Parade.

Although he was born at Clydebank, Gray moved to Bradford with his parents while he was still a child. City spotted him when he was playing for local team Queensbury and he became a full-time professional in David Steele's first season as manager.

Gray made his debut at home to Stockport County in September 1948, but he played only five League matches in each of his first two season. However, he gained a regular place in 1950–51 as an inside-forward in the second half of the campaign, scoring nine goals in 30 League appearances.

He also began the new season at inside-forward, but later he established himself at right-half. Then, former Welsh international half-back Ivor Powell was appointed player-manager, and he found a new position for Gray. He began the season at right-half with Powell playing at left-half, but then Powell moved him to right-back as partner to Jock Whyte, who was essentially a right sided player, but played on the left for half a season. Nonetheless, Gray proved to be an invaluable member of the team as he missed only two matches.

All changed again the following season, when Powell signed George Mulholland on a free transfer from Stoke, and he made the left-back position his own for the next seven seasons, with Whyte switching back to his natural right-back position and Gray playing at right-half.

Gray missed only four League matches that season and, at the end of the campaign, he was awarded a benefit match, when a magnificent crowd of 17,518 turned out to to see the match between Bradford and an All Stars team. One of the 'stars', Welsh international and former Leeds United centre-forward John Charles, who was then playing in Italy, scored a hat-trick to the delight of the paying customers.

Gray had to show his versatility the following season, playing at right-back, right-half, inside-right and inside-left. In fact, he made only six of his 35 League appearances in his natural right-half role after Powell signed Sam Booth from Exeter and Reg Attwell from Burnley who both played in that position.

It was a season of upheaval at Valley Parade, which began with Powell still playing at left-half, but before the end of September he suffered an injury that forced him to retire, and before the end of the campaign he would be gone, to be replaced by Peter Jackson.

The new manager switched Gray back to right-half for the following season, and he was of five ever presents - goalkeeper Geoff Smith, George Mulholland, George Williamson and Johnny Simm were the others.

However, this turned out to Gray's last season in the first team at Valley Parade. He didn't play a single match the following season and was released in March 1957, having made an impressive 242 League appearances plus 15 in the Cup and scoring 13 goals. He later played non-League football with Ossett Town.

John Hall

Date of birth: 18 April 1944

Bradford City record:
Appearances: League 430, FA Cup 21, League Cup 23
Goals: League 63, FA Cup 4, League Cup 5
Debut: 22 September 1962 v Aldershot

Also played for: Gainsborough Trinity, Guiseley, Leeds Ashley Road, Yeadon Celtic
Managed: Yeadon Celtic

Pacy right-winger John Hall clocked up 474 League and Cup appearances in 13 seasons at Valley Parade, making the number-seven shirt his own through most of the 1960s and the first four seasons of the 1970s. Only appearance record holder Ces Podd and Ian Cooper have played more games for the club.

The Bramley-born player ran fast and straight and delivered a good cross so not only did he score 72 League and Cup goals himself, but he provided a stream of opportunities for others to convert into goals.

Hall joined City as an amateur in 1961 after a season with Huddersfield Town, and 12 months later he became a full-time professional. He made his League debut against Aldershot on 22 September 1962, playing 13 League matches that season, when City had to seek re-election for the third time in their history, before becoming a regular player. In fact, such was his consistency – and freedom from injury – that he topped the 40 League appearance record on no fewer than six occasions, playing in every match, including one substitute appearance in what turned out to be his penultimate season – 1972-73.

Hall shared the highs and lows of the 1960s, which included two fifth-place finishes in the Fourth Division in 1963-64 and 1967-68 – the top four were automatically promoted – before playing a key role when City finally did make it back into the Third Division with nine goals in 41 League matches, before they slid back into the Third Division three years later.

Undoubtedly his best season was in 1966-67, also former double international Willie Watson's first full season at Valley Parade. Hall was top scorer with 17 goals in 44 League matches in that campaign. He also made many fine Cup appearances after playing 44 matches in both main competitions. The two most memorable FA Cup ties were the matches against Tottenham Hotspur in 1969-70 and Arsenal in 1972-73. The third-round tie against Spurs drew a 23,000 crowd to Valley Parade on Saturday 3 January 1970, and they were treated to a thriller. Spurs took an early 2-0 lead, but City hit back to level the scores before half-time with an own goal from Welsh international defender Mike England and Bruce Stowell. Then, Hall almost won the game for City 10 minutes from the end, only to see the late Cyril Knowles head out his tremendously struck volley from under the crossbar as the scores finished level at 2-2. It was a different story in the replay at White Hart Lane when Spurs thrashed the Bantams 5-0.

City were drawn away to Arsenal in a fourth round in February 1973, and although they produced a creditable performance they were beaten 2-0, with the second goal being a breakaway from Charlie George.

Hall left City in June 1974 after a testimonial, moving to non-League Gainsborough Trinity in the Northern Premier League, and the following year he signed for Yorkshire League club Guiseley. He then joined Leeds Ashley Road in 1978 and the following year he became player-manager of Yeadon Celtic in the West Riding County Amateur League.

A natural athlete, Hall was also a fine cricketer, playing for the All-England team against the Public Schools at Edgbaston in 1959, and he played Bradford League cricket for Salts and Yeadon.

Tom Hallett

Date of birth: 10 April 1939

Bradford City record:
Appearances: League 179, FA Cup 10, League Cup 11
Goals: League 2
Debut: 20 August 1966 v Southend United

Also played for: Leeds United, Swindon Town

Tom Hallett proved to be a dependable central-defender for five seasons in the late 1960s and early 1970s, as well as being a key member of Bradford City's Fourth Division promotion side. However, the former Welsh Schoolboys captain took a roundabout route to arrive at Valley Parade as he travelled from Wales to Leeds, south west to Swindon and back to West Yorkshire with City.

Frustrated at not being able to break into the Leeds team, Hallett took the chance to move to Swindon in July 1963 and finally made his League debut the following February against Northampton Town, but it took another move back to West Yorkshire before he at last gained a regular place in League football. For he made only 26 appearances in three years at Swindon before manager Willie Watson brought him to Valley Parade in the 1966 close season, in a £1,200 deal, as the former England football and cricket international rebuilt his side after City had suffered the indignity of having to apply for re-election the previous season.

Hallett quickly established himself as a strong, dependable centre-half, playing 29 League matches in his first season as City achieved a respectable 11th place in the table. He did even better the following season as City enjoyed a great first half of season, looking every inch a promotion side.

Hallett was appointed captain for the start of the new campaign, and this time City made sure of promotion, losing only one of their last 21 matches and beating Darlington 3-1 in a crucial final match to clinch fourth place. He was the model of consistency, missing only two League matches, and found himself a new central-defensive partner later in the season. He began the season in partnership with Barry Swallow, but in October 1968 Swallow moved to York City, where he made 269 League appearances and became a director. So, Tony Leighton moved from centre-forward to join Hallett at the heart of the defence and the two of them missed only three matches between them.

Hallett continued to be a dependable player in the Third Division, making 41 League appearances as City finished a disappointing 10th after being in a great position at the turn of the year, and made 19 League appearances in what turned out to be his last season before retiring.

Hallett, who made 200 appearances in five years at Valley Parade – 179 of them in the League – first came to West Yorkshire on the advice of scout Jack Pickard, who sent lots of young Welsh players to Leeds United, including John Charles. In fact, there were 17 Welsh players at Elland Road when Hallett was on the Leeds staff. He captained the junior and reserve sides at Leeds, but achieving a first-team place at centre-half was always going to be difficult because John Charles was there and future England international and World Cup winner Jack Charlton was ready to take over.

After National Service, Hallett thought about going back to Wales, but Swindon manager Bert Head wanted to sign him, and although Norwich also came in for him he joined Swindon, who had a good team in those days with the likes of Don Rogers and Mike Summerbee in the side.

When Head moved to Crystal Palace, Hallett did not get on with new manager Danny Williams. Swansea wanted to sign him, but City manager Willie Watson was also talking to him, and he decided to come to Valley Parade. 'It was a great move for me,' he said, 'and I wish I had come to Bradford earlier – I had the opportunity to go to Bradford before I went to Swindon.' However, he witnessed a tragedy during his spell at City. His former Leeds United teammate Grenville Hair, who had taken over as City manager from Willie Watson, collapsed and died during a training session at Valley Parade, aged just 36. 'He just keeled over as his wife was watching from the office window – she worked at the club. Tony Leighton tried to give him the kiss of life. It was a tragedy – Grenville would have been a good manager,' he said.

Hallett remembers Jimmy McAnearney bringing new ideas into training when he took over as caretaker, but the club appointed Jimmy Wheeler – assistant manager at Reading – as Hair's successor. Wheeler guided City to promotion in his first season, and Hallett said 'He got the best out of players – they respected him.'

Hallett was offered a job on the coaching staff when his playing career was over, but he joined teammate Denis Atkins in a milk delivery business before becoming a PT instructor in the prison service.

Jack Hallows

Date of birth: 1907
Died: August 1963

Bradford City record:
Appearances: League 164, FA Cup 9
Goals: League 74, FA Cup 5
Debut: 22 November 1930 Bradford City v Burnley

Also played for: Grays Thurrocks, Barnsley

Jack Hallows, second from left, in the 1933-34 team photograph.

Jack Hallows was a consistent goalscoring centre-forward for six seasons when Bradford City established themselves as a good class Second Division club after winning promotion back to Division Two in 1929. His 74 League goals in 164 matches place him in third place behind Bobby Campbell and Frank O'Rourke in the club's list of all-time highest goalscorers.

City signed Hallows from the Kent League club Gray's Thurrocks in November 1930 for £600, and what a bargain he proved to be. Hallows, who had a particularly hard shot, was an immediate success, scoring 19 goals in 27 League matches in his first season and 21 in 34 matches in his second season when the club finished seventh. His personal high point that season came when he scored five goals as City hammered Barnsley 9-1 in January 1932. However, his goals began to tail off in his final two seasons at Valley Parade and a two-month suspension imposed by the club after he was sent off in a Midland League match restricted him in his final season.

After scoring 79 League and FA Cup goals in 173 appearances for City, he was transferred to Barnsley in March 1936, but if Barnsley believed that Hallows would repeat the form he showed in scoring five goals against them four years earlier they were to be disappointed; he made only 13 appearances at Oakwell, scoring four goals before retiring.

Hallows had a humble start to life – he was an orphan at St Edmunds in his native Liverpool – but football proved to be a lifeline for him. He played with Liverpool Bluecoats FC where he established his reputation as a goalscorer, and he continued scoring goals for the West Midlands team Willenhall Swifts. He got his first chance of League football with West Bromwich Albion, but his stay at the Hawthorns was disappointing and he was released. Hallows then joined Grays Thurrock from where City gave another chance of League football.

A tailor by trade, Hallows began a bespoke business at Walden near Bolton after retiring from professional football. He died in August 1963.

Bobby Ham

Date of birth: 29 March 1942

Bradford City record:
Appearances: League 188, FA Cup 9, League Cup 11
Goals: League 64, FA Cup 1, League Cup 5
Debut: 17 February 1968 v Crewe Alexandra

Also played for: Bradford Park Avenue, Gainsborough Trinity, Grimsby Town, Preston North End, Rotherham United, Matlock Town, Guiseley
Managed: Gainsborough

Bobby Ham was a natural goalscorer who gave splendid service to Bradford football at both ends of the city and is still playing his part as a director at Valley Parade. In a 14-year career he scored 156 goals in 460 League appearances – an impressive one goal in every three matches – and he has the unique distinction of having played in three separate spells with both Bradford City and Bradford Park Avenue.

After playing with City as a junior, Ham made his League debut for Park Avenue in the 1961–62 season. There followed a brief spell at Grimsby Town before he returned to Park Avenue in 1964 and scored 47 League goals in 134 appearances. He enjoyed his best season in 1965–66 with Park Avenue after forming a lethal partnership with the highly-rated Kevin Hector, who went on to enjoy an illustrious career with Derby County as well as winning two England caps. Despite being the most marked striker in the Fourth Division, Hector scored 44 goals while Ham netted 24.

Ham joined City for a second time in February 1968 in a £2,750 deal – the week aftrer he had scored one of the goals in Avenue's 2–1 win at Valley Parade, which was a blow to the Bantams' promotion hopes. City just missed out on promotion that season, but Ham played a huge part the following season as they made sure of the fourth promotion place with a dramatic 3–1 win at Darlington in the final game. Ham was not the only ever present but was leading scorer with 18 goals, including four goals in a 5–0 home win over York City.

Ham was again the only ever present and also leading scorer the following season – City's first campaign back in the Third Division – with 17 goals, including a hat-trick in the 8–1 home win over Bournemouth. When he was transferred to Preston in October 1970, in a £8,000 deal after scoring 40 goals in 115 League matches for City, he had made 109 consecutive League appearances. He won a Third Division Championship medal at Preston, scoring 14 goals in 43 League matches, before joining Rotherham United. He spent nearly two years at Rotherham, for whom he scored 24 goals in 67 matches, but when they were relegated to the Fourth Division in 1972–73 he re-joined City for a third time. He was top scorer in 1974–75 with 14 goals in 43 matches but was surprisingly given a free transfer at the end of the campaign, having scored 24 goals in 72 appearances in his third and final spell at Valley Parade, before moving into non-League football with Gainsborough Trinity.

Tn the 1969–70 season City met Tottenham Hotspur in an FA Cup third-round tie, and after a 2–2 draw at Valley Parade they lost 5–0 in the replay at White Hart Lane, but Ham caught the eye of Spurs manager Bill Nicholson. His original offer of £25,000 was turned down by City, who asked for £5,000 more. Finally they offered £35,000 plus a player, but again this was rejected by City chairman Stafford Heginbotham, and Spurs lost interest. 'That cost me the chance of First Division football and it is my biggest regret in football,' said Ham. He was also upset that City went back on an agreement that they would increase his wage from £35 to £40. 'They reneged on their promise to increase my pay by £5 at the end of my contract so I asked for a move,' he said. 'So, I left in October 1970 to go to Preston, where I received the £40 I felt I was due at Bradford City.

'Going to Preston was a great move. Archie Gemmill had gone to Derby and I replaced him in the team. They were struggling when I arrived at Deepdale, but we then went unbeaten to the end of February and finished up going to Fulham for their last match of the season. Fulham were already promoted, but needed a point to be champions. We beat them 1–0 and beat Rotherham in our last match to go up as champions. It was like a dream come true, but, halfway through the following season our manager Alan Ball told me the club had decided to let me go. 'You are 30 and we are looking for younger players,' he said.

'So, I joined Rotherham and I had two good years there before Bryan Edwards signed me for City to finish my career at Valley Parade. When I left City I could have gone to Scunthorpe as player-manager, but I was in business with my brother Alan so I decided to go into the business full time.

'I joined Gainsborough Trinity, but I only played a few games for them when I suffered a double fracture of the leg and I was out of action for 11 and a half months. It was an injury that finished my football career, but I took up rugby union and played for Cleckheaton and Baildon until I was 52. I loved rugby – in fact, I love any sport.'

Ham is now back at Valley Parade as a director of the club following the 2004 administration crisis, helping with commercial activities.

Joe Hargreaves

Date of birth: 1890
Died: June 1924

Bradford City record:
Appearances: League 188, FA Cup 15
Goals: League 6
Debut: 14 February 1912 v Bolton Wanderers

Also played for: Great Harwood, Accrington Stanley

Born in the Lancashire town of Enfield in 1890, Hargreaves began his career with Clayton YMCA before playing for Great Harwood and Accrington Stanley and it was from Accrington that City signed for a nominal £65 fee in December 1911, six months after they won the FA Cup.

Hargreaves began his Valley Parade career before the war, making his first appearances in 1911–12 – the season after City won the FA Cup – and his Valley Parade career spanned 12 seasons, including four in wartime when League football was suspended.

Hargreaves joined City at the time that manager Peter O'Rourke was beginning to re-cast and rejuvenate the team. City were a leading First Division club in those days, and the 1911–12 season will be remembered for the great effort to retain the Cup. Unfortunately, they were beaten in a dramatic quarter-final by the eventual winners Barnsley after two replays.

Although Hargreaves made five appearances in his first season, it was not until the 1914–15 campaign that he gained a regular place in the side, playing in 33 League and Cup matches. The war was not expected to last and so at first League football continued as normal during the hostilities. It was only when it was realised that it was going to be a much longer campaign than people realised that the competition was suspended.

That was frustrating for players of Hargreaves's generation, who reached their peak during the war, but he made 64 appearances in the four wartime seasons, and when League football resumed in 1919 he was a key member of the side as City began their ultimately unsuccessful effort to preserve their First Division status.

Changes were inevitable, and the half-back line of right-half Hargreaves, centre-half Charlie Storer and left-half Donald Duckett first came together in the fourth match of the 1919–20 – a 1–1 draw at Burnley. Storer, who began his career as a centre-forward, moved to the centre of defence to replace Bob Torrance after the FA Cup Final hero was killed in action in 1917, while Duckett, who made his debut in wartime football, claimed a regular place when hostilities ended.

Hargreaves was a hard working player, who was a great favourite with players and supporters alike. He missed only three matches in 1919–20 and four the following season. He also made 29 League appearances in 1921–22 – the season City were relegated – and he continued to be a regular during the following campaign after City dropped back into the Second Division.

He made just seven appearances in the 1923–24 season and everyone was shocked when he was tragically killed in a motorcycle accident at Cleckheaton in June 1924, aged 34.

Hargreaves, who made 188 League appearances for City, scoring six goals and 15 FA Cup appearances, was also a noted all-round League cricketer with Spen Victoria in the Yorkshire Council.

Derek Hawksworth

Date of birth: 16 July 1927

Bradford City record:
Appearances: League 119, FA Cup 8, League Cup 1
Goals: League 28, FA Cup 1
Debut: 21 August 1948 v Barrow

Also played for: Sheffield United, Huddersfield Town, Lincoln City, Nelson

Derek Hawksworth enjoyed his best years away from Bradford, but he will be remembered as one of the best footballers the city has produced. A tall winger or inside-forward, the versatile Hawksworth played top-level football with Sheffield United in the mid-1950s, but his path to League football was anything but smooth.

He was born in the Manningham district of Bradford in 1927 and was playing for Manningham Mills under-16s when he joined Park Avenue as a 14-year-old in the early years of the war, when future City boss David Steele was manager. Steele's successor Fred Emery wanted Hawksworth to work in the mines as a Bevin Boy like some other Avenue players, but he said 'I decided against it and joined the RAF. I had been in the air force for only three weeks, stationed at Wilmslow, when venue asked if I could be released to play for Manchester City at Maine Road.' He played for Avenue's nursery club, Bradford United, in the Yorkshire League and was in the RAF for three years, two of them in India, before he came home in 1947.

Hawksworth signed for Huddersfield Town as an amateur before joining City, where Steele had just been appointed manager. He recalls 'I went to Bradford City because Steele was there. I was an electrician by trade and trained at Valley Parade in the evenings - sometimes there was only me there. David Steele said "You don't seem to be playing as well as you can play." I told him "I don't see the ball - I am only running round the ground." So Steele said "I think you will improve a lot if you go full-time." I said "I will go full-time if I can work in the afternoon." So, I continued my work as an electrician, training in the morning and working in the afternoon for Collinson Brothers, where one of the partners was a City supporter, Geoff Collinson, and that was the pattern until I was transferred to Sheffield United.'

Hawksworth made his City debut in a 0-0 draw at Barrow on the opening day of the 1948-49 season and established himself as a regular player, making 33 League and Cup appearances and scoring seven goals. The highlight was City's 4-2 home win over Hull City, the Third Division North glamour club in front of the highest post-war crowd at Valley Parade - 27,083 - in February 1949, but it was a rare flash of brilliance in a drab season as City were forced to apply for re-election for the first time in their history.

Hawksworth made 26 League appearances with four goals the following season and enjoyed a rich vein of form the season after that with 10 goals in the first 19 matches. His performances began to attract the scouts and it was no surprise when he moved midway through that season, his third season at Valley Parade - in December 1950 - to Sheffield United for City's record incoming fee of £12,500, the week after he scored a hat-trick in their 5-3 home win against Wrexham.

The move to Bramall Lane was a huge success for Hawksworth. He scored 88 goals in 255 League appearances for United in undoubtedly the best period of his career, and a key feature of his eight years with the Blades was his partnership with inside-left Jimmy Hagan - one of the best inside-forwards of his generation.

Hawksworth also won some representative honours during his spell at Sheffield United, playing for an FA XI against The Army at Highbury in November 1951 and winning an England B cap against France at Le Havre in May 1952. More importantly, the following season he won a Second Division Championship medal with United and played for three seasons in the top division before he was transferred to Huddersfield Town in exchange for Ronnie Simpson plus £6,000.

In his two seasons at Huddersfield, he played alongside Scottish international Denis Law before he was transferred to Lincoln City, where David Steele signed him for the third time. He returned to City in January 1961 for a £3,000 fee, but he could not help them to avoid relegation to the Fourth Division and left in July 1962 to go to non-League Nelson, where he finished his career.

Stafford Heginbotham

Died: April 1995

Bradford City record:
Chairman: 1965–1973 and 1983–1987

Larger than life character Stafford Heginbotham helped to rescue Bradford City not once, but twice during an association with the club spanning more than 20 years. The Lancashire-born businessman, who died in 1995, was twice chairman of City, coming to their rescue in 1965 and again in 1983 when City spent two months in receivership.

On the field, he shared in the joys of promotion from the old Fourth Division in 1969 and the old Third Division Championship triumph of 1985 and also guided the club through the aftermath of the fire disaster and the rebuilding of the Valley Parade ground.

In a sport where conventions tend to be slavishly followed, Stafford was a man of ideas – not all of them feasible, but always original. He devised a club emblem – the City Gent with bowler hat and rolled umbrella – which lasted for many years, established a nightclub near Valley Parade and developed ideas like inviting supporters to be directors for a day to boost income and create interest in the football club.

Stafford Heginbotham's name was little known to the public of Bradford before October 1965, when he and his solicitor friend George Ide took over the club when they were in dire straits both on and off the field. After narrowly escaping having to apply for re-election the season before, City had lost eight of their first 11 matches, including successive humiliating 7-1 thrashings against Crewe away and Stockport at home in the September and a 5-1 defeat by Rochdale. They had little or no money and the chairman, timber merchant Albert Harris, was ready to quit.

Stafford's widow Lorna recalls that Albert Harris had put a piece in the paper outlining the club's plight. 'George Ide was at our house, we had a few drinks when he and Stafford said to each "Why don't we take over this club." I left the room because I thought they were drunk, but the following day Stafford came back home and said "We have been down to see him to take over the club." Albert Harris resigned – it was as simple as that.'

Stafford – friend and foe alike knew him by his distinctive Christian name – became the youngest chairman in the Football League at 33, and the new board immediately provided money for manager Bill Harris to make new signings. The most eye-catching newcomer was Harris's fellow Welsh international Ken Leek, who joined City for a record £10,000, but despite the influx of new players there was no revival as City had to seek re-election for the third time in their history, and it would be four more years before City would gain promotion under Jimmy Wheeler after narrowly missing out the season before.

Two years into his chairmanship, Stafford needed to appeal to supporters for more investment, and he called a meeting at St George's Hall. Some 2,000 fans packed into Bradford's premier concert venue and were treated to a brilliant one-man show as Stafford held the stage for two hours, answering questions and outlining ways in which supporters could help the club.

Two years later City gained promotion under Jimmy Wheeler after making sure of fourth place with a thrilling last-match win at Darlington, and to raise some much needed cash for team strengthening Stafford controversially sold Valley Parade to Bradford Council in 1970 for £35,000, with the club paying an annual rent of £3,500. Unfortunately, the two players City bought with the proceeds, Colin Hall and Terry Owen, did not measure up, and after that City were relegated back to the Third Division.

Stafford resigned in October 1973, a year after relegation, giving way as chairman to new board member Bob Martin, but in his 10 years away from Valley Parade he kept in touch with football by becoming a commentator for BBC Radio Leeds. It was new to him, but he tackled the job with relish. He was also in demand as an after-dinner speaker, where his eloquence and quick-witted repartee entertained audiences sporting and otherwise. Stafford never lost interest in City's affairs, and when the club went into receivership in 1983 he was quickly back on the scene in partnership with Jack Tordoff.

Stafford's energy and drive played no small part in City's Third Division Championship triumph in 1985, two years after they survived receivership. However, less than an hour after receiving the Championship trophy at the last match of the season, triumph turned to tragedy when the Valley Parade stand was engulfed by fire and 56 people lost their lives. Rubbish under the seats in the stand had caught fire, and the club did not escape criticism in the inquiries that followed the disaster, but Stafford shared in the grief of the victims' families by attending as many funerals as possible.

Stafford had a heart attack in 1985, just months before the fire, and decided to retire from the board for health reasons in December 1987. He continued to suffer from ill health and died in April 1995 after a heart transplant operation.

John Hendrie

Date of birth: 24 October 1963

Bradford City record:
Appearances: League 173, FA Cup 11, League Cup 17
Goals: League 46, FA Cup 6, League Cup 3
Debut: 25 August 1984 v Cambridge United

Also played for: Coventry City, Hereford United (loan), Newcastle United, Leeds United, Middlesbrough, Barnsley
Managed: Barnsley

Bradford City can have made few better free transfer signings than John Hendrie, who joined them in June 1984 from Coventry City. The Scottish youth international winger or striker was one of two key signings City made that close season – defender Dave Evans from Halifax Town was the other – as player-manager Trevor Cherry built his promotion team.

Such was Hendrie's consistency that he missed only one League match in four seasons, and he became one of the most popular players of an era that is fondly remembered by City supporters.

A pacy winger who liked to cut in and shoot, Hendrie added a valuable dimension to City's team, not just in the traditional winger skills of beating defenders and supplying accurate passes and crosses, but he was also one of the side's leading goalscorers. He was a key member of the side that won the Third Division Championship in his first season when he was second leading scorer to Bobby Campbell with nine goals, and he was then joint top scorer with Campbell after 10 goals in City's first season back in the Second Division, top scorer with 14 goals in 1986-87 and second leading scorer to Ron Futcher in 1987-88, when City missed out on automatic promotion before losing to Middlesbrough in the Play-off semi-finals.

After City failed in their attempt to win promotion in the spring of 1988, it was inevitable that their two best players, Hendrie and Stuart McCall, would leave to fulfil their ambitions of playing in the top flight. So McCall went to Everton in a £850,000 deal, and Hendrie moved to Newcastle for £500,000 during the close season.

He left Valley Parade with the impressive record of 59 League and Cup goals in 212 appearances, including 46 in 173 League games. The only match he missed was the final game of 1987-88, which proved to be his last season with the club – he was suspended after being harshly sent off at Manchester City three weeks before.

Without him, City lost 3-2 at home to Ipswich, a match they needed to win to secure automatic promotion. Would the presence of Hendrie have made a difference? Who knows, but given Hendrie's outstanding record they would have had a much better chance of winning this vital match.

Hendrie made 34 League appearances, scoring four goals in one season, at St James' Park before moving back to West Yorkshire with Leeds United. After a season at Elland Road, where he scored five goals in 27 League matches, he was on the move again to Middlesbrough where he enjoyed a successful six-year spell, scoring 44 goals in 192 League appearances.

In the autumn of 1996 the then City manager Chris Kamara tried to bring Hendrie back to Valley Parade on loan, but Barnsley moved in with a £250,000 offer and Hendrie helped them to win promotion to the Premiership. Unfortunately, they lasted only one season in the top flight, and when manager Danny Wilson, who had guided them to promotion, moved to Sheffield Wednesday, Hendrie was appointed player-manager. He gradually wound down his playing career as he concentrated on his managerial duties, and when he was sacked by Barnsley he retired from the game with a fine record of 518 League appearances and 108 goals.

Hendrie, who is a regular visitor to Valley Parade, helping BBC Radio Leeds with their commentaries, has great affection for his old club. 'Going to City was a fantastic move,' he said. 'I had been on loan to Hereford that season – 1983-84 – and I knew I would be leaving in the summer. I spoke to Port Vale and a couple of Scottish clubs, but Greg Abbott, who had been an apprentice with me at Coventry, sold Bradford City to me.'

Hendrie said that, when he left Barnsley, Brighton, Blackpool and Burnley were among the clubs interested in signing him, but he fractured a bone in his hand while playing in the Masters competition. His hand was in plaster for five months and he had to have a bone graft, so he decided to retire. 'If I could have kept my fitness levels going I would have played a lot longer. I was 35 and I wanted to play for another two or three years,' he said.

Hendrie now works for solicitors Last Cawthra, helping football clients with contracts and legal problems, while also doing commentary work for BBC Radio Leeds. Two of his sons, Jordan (under-11s) and Luke (under-13s), play for City's youth sides.

George Hinsley

Date of birth: 19 July 1914
Died: March 1989

Bradford City record:
Appearances: League 114, FA Cup 6
Goals: League 17, FA Cup 1
Debut: 19 November 1938 v Rotherham United

Also played for: Barnsley, Halifax Town, Nelson
Managed: Farsley Celtic

George Hinsley was one of hundreds of League footballers whose careers were blighted by World War Two. Many years later he also reflected on the heavy toll that the war inflicted on Bradford City, recalling that only three players from their pre-war team – Spud Murphy, Alf Whittingham and himself – returned to the club when hostilities ended, which meant that City had to recruit a new team when League football resumed in 1946 after a seven year gap.

Born at Sheffield, he played for Yorkshire schoolboys in 1927-28 and had trials at Denaby United and Fulham before joining Sheffield Wednesday. He stayed at Hillsborough for four years before signing for Barnsley in September 1935. Although he played only nine League matches with Barnsley, he did play in a sixth-round FA Cup tie against Arsenal at Highbury in February 1936 in front of a crowd of 60,420, as deputy for the famous Pongo Waring.

After failing to gain a regular first-team place at Oakwell, he moved to Bradford City in October 1938 in part exchange for left-back Gordon Pallister, with Barnsley also paying City a £1,250 cash balance. After a long career as a regular player at Oakwell, where he made 220 League appearances, Pallister became a Barnsley director while Hinsley achieved a regular place at City as a central-defender, half-back and inside-forward.

Hinsley told me of his first impressions of Valley Parade. Facilities in those days were antiquated. The dressing rooms were really cellars of the bottom two houses in Burlington Terrace, one of which served as the club offices until the present dressing room block was built at the opposite end of the main stand in 1960. The staircase had to be negotiated with great difficulty and above the dressing room was a gymnasium. He recalls 'It was late afternoon when I came to sign and I was sitting in the dressing room. Suddenly the cellar door blew open and the trainer Harold Peel looked at me and said "Don't panic, it is Dickie Bond's ghost."'

Hinsley, who joined City 18 months after they were relegated from the Second Division, believes the club had a good chance of promotion midway through the 1938-39 season. He recalls 'We were in the top at Christmas and Barnsley were close to us. We played them at Valley Parade and the ground was frozen. I felt we were wrongly set up that day and in consequence our football became tentative rather than competitive, whereas they seemed to be able to keep their feet better. In the end, we finished third that season. It was said we would have walked away with the Third Division North had the war not intervened.'

Although he spent 11 years at Valley Parade, Hinsley lost seven seasons to the war, during which he served as an RAF PE sergeant instructor and guested for Liverpool, Birmingham and Walsall, as well as making 80 appearances for City. He had the unusual distinction of scoring City's last goal before the war – a 2-2 draw at Barrow the day before war broke out – and their first goal in a 3-1 home win over Accrington Stanley when League football resumed in 1946.

Hinsley was a regular player in the first two seasons after the war and, as a natural leader, he became captain, but he lost his place in the 1948-49 season and was transferred at the end of the campaign to Halifax Town for £400. After one season at Halifax he moved into non-League football with Nelson and later spent eight years as manager and coach to Farsley Celtic during the 1950s, when Celtic were a Yorkshire League side.

It is a pity that George did not go into professional coaching and management when his playing days were over to pass on his knowledge and enthusiasm, but he spent the rest of his life doing his best to provide opportunities for young people to play the game he loved, and, in his work as an educational welfare officer for Bradford Council, to improve the way of life for the families and young people of his adopted city. He also coached several local sides, among which was Trinity Athletic, where he became chairman. He was also founder chairman of the Bradford Youth Evening Floodlit League playing at Myra Shay near the Bradford Moor area of the city.

The League established an all-weather shale pitch at Myra Shay, using Bradford City's original floodlights from 1955. Happily, all-weather pitches with artificial grass and good quality floodlights are common nowadays, but that was not the case in the 1960s and the all-weather pitch at Myra Shay and the youth floodlit League enabled young footballers to train and play in good conditions during the winter. George Hinsley died in March 1989, aged 74.

Don Hutchins

Date of birth: 8 May 1948

Bradford City record:
Appearances: League 256, FA Cup 14, League Cup 16
Goals: League 44, FA Cup 5, League Cup 3
Debut: 17 August 1974 v Crewe Alexandra

Also played for: Middlesbrough, Leicester City, Plymouth Argyle, Blackburn Rovers

Many teams nowadays long for a genuine left-sided player in defence or attack. Well, for the second half of the 1970s City had just that player. Don Hutchins was a skilful left-winger, who could beat defenders and deliver a good cross while scoring goals as well. In seven years at Valley Parade he scored 44 goals in 256 appearances.

Hutchins, who was born in Middlesbrough, was an able schoolboy footballer, who played with the North Riding and Middlesbrough Boys teams and joined his home-town club when former England international Raich Carter was manager. He also played junior football for neighbouring Stockton-on-Tees, but he had to move away from his native Teeside to break into League football. So, he signed for Leicester City and made his debut in a First Division match at Burnley in April 1968. Unfortunately, he could not command a regular place at Filbert Street, and after making just four League appearances he joined Plymouth Argyle in July 1969 for £6,000.

The move to the West Country gave Hutchins the chance to establish himself in regular first-team football, and he made 95 League appearances in three years and was also leading scorer in 1970–71. Hutchins moved to Blackburn Rovers in July 1972 but never commanded a regular place, making 40 League appearances over two years before he joined City.

Manager Bryan Edwards knew Hutchins from his time as assistant manager at Plymouth and decided to bring him to Valley Parade in the 1974 close season in part exchange for defender or midfield player Graham Oates, with City receiving a cash balance of £10,000 as part of the deal.

Hutchins immediately became a key member of City's mid-table Fourth Division, missing only three matches in his first season. He helped City to reach the FA Cup quarter-finals the following season, scoring five goals in six matches before they were beaten at Valley Parade by the eventual winners Southampton.

In that season he also became the first City player to win a PFA nomination for a divisional team when they chose him for their Fourth Division side, and he said 'It was great to be chosen by your fellow professionals, and I enjoyed going to the Hilton Hotel in London to receive the awards'.

However, his best season came a year later when he scored 14 goals in 44 League games as City gained promotion to the Third Division under manager Bobby Kennedy.

Hutchins missed only one match, scoring nine goals as City were relegated the following season, and continued his consistency back in the Fourth Division with 37 League appearances. However, he missed 19 matches in 1979–80, as City suffered the heartbreak of missing out on promotion by the narrowest of margins under George Mulhall, and he played only 22 matches the following season before leaving the club and calling time on a League career that saw him make 397 League appearances and score 73 goals.

Hutchins said 'I wouldn't have come to Bradford but for Bryan Edwards, who was my coach at Plymouth. It would have spoiled the Graham Oates transfer to Blackburn if I had turned down the move to Bradford, but I am pleased I came to Valley Parade. In fact, out of the clubs I played for I enjoyed my time at Bradford the most. Even though I am a Middlesbrough lad, I always took Bradford to my heart.

'The promotion season stands out in my mind, and I remember the celebrations in the city and going to the Lord Mayor's reception. I believe we should have strengthened the team after gaining promotion. Defensively we were not good enough. We were alright up front, but we let in too many goals and we came back down.

'The other highlight was the FA Cup run when we reached the quarter-finals. I remember I scored against Chesterfield to get us through the first round and then went to Rotherham where we played really well to win 3–0. That was our best performance. After beating Shrewsbury in the third round, we were drawn against the London non-League club Tooting and Mitcham, who thought they would beat us, but I scored twice and we won 3–1'

That set City up for a fifth-round tie at Norwich. The match was delayed because of a flu epidemic, which provoked some disparaging comments from Norwich manager John Bond about whether lower division clubs should be taking part in the FA Cup and Hutchins said 'After all that John Bond said it was nice to get one over them. It was a night to remember as we beat them 2–1. I know we soaked up a lot of pressure, but it was a night to remember and the supporters were fantastic. Billy McGinley, who scored the winner, should have passed to Gerry Ingram, but his shot rebounded to him, and he shot through goalkeeper Kevin Keelan's legs. We were unlucky to lose against Southampton in the quarter-final and the goal they scored would probably be disallowed now. Peter Osgood flicked up the ball for Jim McCalliog to score.'

After retiring from football, Hutchins worked for Leyland paint company and became regional sales manager. He is now retired.

Gerry Ingram

Date of birth: 19 August 1947

Bradford City record
Appearances: League 174, FA Cup 17, League Cup 8
Goals: League 60, FA Cup 8
Debut: 4 March 1972 v Bournemouth

Also played for: Blackpool, Preston North End

It was not a successful era in Bradford City's history, but centre-forward Gerry Ingram excelled in a five-year spell at Valley Parade in the mid-1970s. The blond, strongly-built Ingram joined City just before the transfer deadline in March 1972, along with his Preston teammates left-back John Ritchie and right-winger David Wilson, as the club made a determined but failed bid to avoid relegation from the Third Division.

Ingram was born in Hull in 1947 and played for the city boys team before playing for Hull City Juniors, Hall Road Rangers and Hull Brunswick in the Yorkshire League. It was his goalscoring record for Hull Brunswick that attracted the attention of League clubs and Blackpool paid £1,000 for him in 1967. He was an immediate success at Bloomfield Road and scored 18 goals in his first full season at Blackpool, but it was not quite enough to help the club into the Second Division.

Such was his success at Blackpool, that their neighbours Preston signed him in September 1968 for £27,000 and he played a big part in their promotion to the Second Division in 1970-71 with 22 goals, which made him the Third Division's joint top scorer, and he played another season at Deepdale before joining City.

The experienced Wilson, who had enjoyed two fine spells at Preston with an unsuccessful spell at Liverpool in between, arrived on loan, but Ingram and Ritchie cost City a combined total of £20,000 – a big deal for the club in those days.

The hope was that Ingram would solve City's chronic goalscoring problems, but unfortunately these bold signings had no impact at all as the Bantams lost 13 of their last 20 matches, winning just three. Ingram scored three in 16, including two in a remarkable 4-1 win at Plymouth, but City suffered the indignity of finishing bottom of Division Three.

During the summer, manager Bryan Edwards signed another strong centre-forward, the tall Allan Gilliver, and he and Ingram formed a successful striking partnership, scoring 35 League and Cup goals between them – Gilliver 20 and Ingram 15 – but City finished a disappointing 16th and the highlights came in the FA Cup.

There Ingram had the personal satisfaction of scoring both goals in the 2-1 third-round win over his old club Blackpool – then in the Second Division, two divisions above City – in front of a 14,205 crowd – three times the average League gate at Valley Parade in those Fourth Division days. City then lost 2-0 at Arsenal in front of a 40,407 crowd at Highbury, a solo goal by Charlie George midway through the second half sealing the Gunners' victory after a brave effort by the Bantams.

The Ingram-Gilliver partnership was also successful the following season, with Ingram top scoring with 18 League and Cup goals, while Gilliver scored 12, as City again reached the FA Cup Fourth Round and finished eighth in the League. Surprisingly, City sold Gilliver to Stockport during the close season, and Bobby Ham, who had returned to Valley Parade from Preston the season before, became Ingram's striking partner. Ham was City's top scorer with 14 League goals, while Ingram scored 11 as City finished 10th and notched 10 the following season plus two in the FA Cup as City reached the quarter-final the first time for 56 years, but they were beaten at home by the eventual winners Southampton in front of 14,195 and the Match of the Day cameras.

Ingram scored nine more goals the following season as City won promotion back to the Third Division, but he left before the end of the campaign to play in the US, having scored 68 goals in 199 League and Cup appearances, including 60 in 174 matches in the League. After a loan period with Washington Diplomats, he joined the NASL club permanently in February 1977 for a £4,000 fee and settled in the States when his football career was over.

So, he was lost to English football at the age of 29, but he could look back with satisfaction on a fine League record of roughly one goal in every three matches – 117 in 317.

David Jackson

Date of birth: 23 January 1937

Bradford City record:
Appearances: League 250, FA Cup 23, League Cup 2
Goals: League 61, FA Cup 7
Debut: 20 April 1955 v Grimsby Town

Also played for: Wrexham, Tranmere Rovers, Halifax Town, Frickley Colliery, Alrincham, Hyde United

When Bradford City appointed Peter Jackson as manager in February 1955, they also acquired two new players, the manager's 18-year-old twin sons David and Peter. David, a former England youth international, was a tall inside-forward, who liked to play the long, accurate, defence splitting pass while scoring his share of goals, and by the time he left the club in 1961 he had scored 61 goals in 250 League matches while playing in 25 Cup games and scoring seven goals – a proud record of 68 goals in 275 League and Cup games.

David made his League debut in October 1954 as an amateur for Wrexham, where his father was manager, before playing with Lancashire Combination club Marine. He rejoined his father at City in March 1955 and played for two years as an amateur before becoming a part-time professional in July 1957, combining football with his architectural studies.

David was a regular for the next six seasons as his father built a good class Third Division club, laced with some great FA Cup matches. He was an ever present in 1957-58 when City finished third in the last season of the regional Third Division, missing out on promotion but booking their place in the national Third Division, and missed only one match the following season as City finished 11th.

David played 40 League matches in 1959-60 as well as eight FA Cup games as City reached the fifth round. He scored one of the goals against Everton as City beat the First Division side 3-0 at Valley Parade in the third round before being knocked out in a fifth-round replay at Turf Moor by Burnley, who went on to win the First Division Championship.

His City career ended the following season when his father was sacked as manager in March 1961, six years after he joined the club. The club were heading towards relegation, and the directors did what all directors have done through the years and still do today – sack the manager.

Neither David nor Peter played for City again after their father left the club and at the end of the season they were transferred to Tranmere Rovers for a combined fee of £3,000. David spent two seasons at Tranmere, making 38 League appearances and two more seasons at Halifax Town, where he played 66 League games before calling time on his League career.

David then played non-League football with Frickley Colliery, Altrincham and Hyde United before retiring in 1968 to concentrate on his career as an architect. He also excelled at cricket and golf. David is a long-standing member of West Bradford Golf Club, where he has been captain and also president of the Bradford Golf Union. He played Bradford League cricket with Salts and Great Horton and with Scholes in the Yorkshire Council.

'We tried to think we contributed something to Bradford City,' he said, 'and, with a bit of luck, we might have gone up. Unfortunately, having failed to go up the team broke up. I played inside-right and John Reid played inside-left, and although we scored a smattering of goals we were mainly providers, and wingers like Bobby Webb also scored goals. In fact, we were all expected to score goals.

'I suppose the difference between then and now is that we were less cautious. Nowadays everyone is frightened of making mistakes. Also, if you touch a player now he just falls over. We had a good team spirit in those days. Everyone lived locally.'

David said other clubs made inquiries about them, but they decided to stay at Valley Parade. They also decided against going full-time to concentrate on their respective professions. 'If we had gone full-time, as we could have done, we could have moved on, but football is a very risky business,' he said.

David enjoyed his non-League career, notably with Altrincham under that great character Freddie Pye who became a director of Manchester City. At that time, Altrincham were the glamour side of non-League football in the north, along with Wigan Athletic. David recalls reaching the fourth round of the FA Cup with them and is convinced that under the current feeder system they would have become a League club.

Peter Jackson

Date of birth: 23 January 1937
Died: 1991

Bradford City record:
Appearances: League 199, FA Cup 15, League Cup 34
Goals: League 15, League Cup 1
Debut: 30 April 1955 v Grimsby Town

Also played for: Wrexham, Tranmere Rovers, Frickley Colliery, Alrincham, Hyde United, Macclesfield Town, Guiseley

Peter was a hard working, hard tackling defensive style half-back, a workhorse without whom no team can succeed. His career matched that of his twin brother David.

Peter made his League debut as an amateur playing alongside his brother for Wrexham against Carlisle United at the Racecourse Ground in October 1954. Both brothers also played with the Merseyside club Crosby before joining City with David when their father became manager at Valley Parade in March 1955.

Peter made his City debut in a 4-1 win at Grimsby in April 1955 and held a regular place over the next six years, apart from when he broke a leg in a home match against Southampton in December 1959, just as City's famous FA Cup run was beginning to gather pace.

City had beaten Rochdale in a second-round replay three days before to set up a third-round home tie against First Division Everton and did not play again until the start of the following season, which proved to be his last at Valley Parade. So, he missed the memorable 3-0 win over Everton and the two matches against Burnley, who knocked City out of the competition after a fifth-round replay at Turf Moor.

After their father was sacked in March 1961 the brothers joined Tranmere Rovers for a combined fee of £3,000. David left after two years at Prenton Park to join Halifax Town, but Peter stayed for another two years, became captain and developed into a centre-half.

In the 1965 close season, he teamed up with David at Frickley Colliery, and they played together at Altrincham and Hyde United before Peter decided to extend his career at Macclesfield and Guiseley.

Peter made 199 League appearances for City, scoring 15 goals and was an ever present in 1957–58 and missed only three matches the following season. He also played 15 FA matches. He made 81 League appearances for Tranmere and, together with the seven matches he played for Wrexham, he made a total of 287 League appearances for his three clubs.

Like his brother, he was only ever a part-time professional choosing to pursue his career as an accountant and, like, David he was also an accomplished golfer and cricketer.

Both he and David were active members of the Bradford City and Park Avenue Ex-Players' Association. Peter was also treasurer and one of the prime organisers of the annual dinner. He was only 54 when he died in 1991.

Peter Jackson and his twin brother David, with the rest of the Bradford team, take a break in training to listen to instruction from the manager, Peter Jackson, who was their father.

Peter Jackson

Date of birth: 6 April 1961

Bradford City record:
Appearances: League 336, FA Cup 15, League Cup 34
Goals: League 29, League Cup 1
Debut: 11 April 1979 v Torquay United

Also played for: Newcastle United, Huddersfield Town, Chester City
Managed: Huddersfield Town (twice)

Peter Jackson will always a have a special place in Bradford City's history. Only six players in the 104-year history of the club have played in more League matches – he made 336 League appearances as a committed central-defender in two spells at Valley Parade.

The club's youngest-ever captain – he was made skipper at 19 – he led City to the Third Division Championship in 1985 and is much admired for the way he conducted himself as skipper during the trauma and aftermath of the Valley Parade fire tragedy.

Born in Bradford but brought up in Keighley, he was signed as a schoolboy by Burnley, but he was released and joined City as a 16-year-old in 1977 and became a full-time professional in April 1979, on the same day as his friend Barry Gallagher – they had birthdays on successive days. Manager George Mulhall gave him his first-team debut in a 3–1 defeat at Hereford, and he made eight appearances that season -1978-79.

The central-defensive partnership of Steve Baines and Terry Cooper kept him out of the side for the first half of the following season – the season that City missed promotion on goal average – but he played in the last 11 matches and established himself the following season, missing only one match.

At the end of that season, City signed former England defender Roy McFarland, and during the season defender Joe Cooke returned to the club, so the three of them shared defensive duties as City gained promotion. Still, Jackson made 30 League appearances and gained a regular place the following season after McFarland unexpectedly left to go back to Derby County.

The following season, he had another England international, new player-manager Trevor Cherry, as his central-defensive partner as he made 42 appearances. Cherry then signed Dave Evans from Halifax Town, and he and Jackson formed the central-defensive partnership that led them to the Third Division title.

Their consistency was a crucial element in City's Championship triumph – each missed only one match – but then City's title triumph turned to tragedy. Jackson led his teammates on a lap of honour round Valley Parade after receiving the Championship trophy just before the last match of the season against Lincoln City, but just before half-time fire engulfed the main stand and 56 people lost their lives.

The tragedy overshadowed what had been a memorable season as promotion returned City to the Second Division for the first time for 48 years. Jackson said 'The season had been a tremendous one for us. We were the comeback side. We never gave in. Such was the spirit and the feeling of togetherness when we never contemplated defeat even if we went a goal down'.

Jackson went straight from Valley Parade to visit the hundreds of people who had been taken to Bradford Royal Infirmary for treatment to burns and other injuries, and in the weeks after the fire he attended funerals of the victims, visited the sick and organised for the players to do visits and attend fundraising events.

Jackson was an ever present the following season as City established themselves in the Second Division despite playing all their matches away from a fire-wrecked Valley Parade. City led a nomadic existence as they played their 'home' games at Bradford's Odsal Stadium, Leeds United and Huddersfield Town, but before City could go back to Valley Parade Jackson got his big move – a £250,000 transfer to Newcastle United in October 1986.

Jackson had two seasons in the top flight with Newcastle, winning the club's Player of the Year award before he made an unexpected return to City in a £290,000 deal in September 1988. He made another 58 League appearances for the club, but the move was not a success, as Jackson admitted, 'It never worked out for me', he said. 'My biggest regret is that I came back and let so many people down'.

It was a relief to both club and player when he moved to Huddersfield Town on a free transfer in September 1990 – City wanted to reduce their wage bill after being relegated, while Jackson wanted a fresh start. Going to Huddersfield turned out to be a good move for Jackson – a club he was to manage later in his career. He made 155 League appearances in four seasons before ending his career with Chester, where he played a further 100 League matches before retiring.

When Jackson returned to the club in July 2003, Town had dropped two divisions to the fourth tier of English football and were in administration. At his first training session he had only eight players to work with, but, despite this unpromising start, he guided Town to promotion by the Play-offs in his first season. The following season, Town finished a point outside the Play-offs and the season after that they reached them only to be beaten by the eventual winners, Yorkshire rivals Barnsley.

Jackson could have been manager of Bradford City in December 2001 when Jim Jefferies left the club. He met the chairman Geoffrey Richmond, but he wasn't 100 percent certain he should take the job. Later he said he had no regrets about turning it down, although he was flattered to be asked.

Peter Jackson (manager)

Date of birth: 4 August 1904
Died: 9 May 1986

Bradford City record
Manager: 1955–1961

Played for: Stoke City, Congleton, Southend United
Also managed: Wrexham

After the slump in form during the last six months of Ivor Powell's management, Bradford City turned to the steady, experienced hand of Peter Jackson to guide them. Jackson's appointment marked the start of a largely successful six-year spell at Valley Parade, but first he had to make sure City managed to avoid having to seek re-election.

Jackson moved to Valley Parade a month after he had parted company with Wrexham, where he had been manager for four and a half years, and he brought with him his 18-year-old twin sons David and Peter, who were to play a big part in a long spell at the club.

City made a great start under Powell, winning five of their first seven matches, but they slumped after the injury that ended his playing career and at one stage they won only twice in a 17-match spell in the middle of the season – a miserable run that led to Powell's departure. There was no dramatic improvement under Jackson, but he guided them to five victories in the last two months of the season, including a double over Grimsby – 4–0 at home, 4–1 away – and they finished fourth from the bottom.

A feature of Jackson's management style was his shrewd business in the transfer market. There was little money for transfer fees, and so Jackson signed up to 10 free transfer players in the close season hoping that four or five of them would become first-team regulars of the side.

Powell had put his faith in older players like the Burnley pair Jackie Chew and Reg Attwell, Billy Tunnicliffe, Tom Mycock, Jock Kirton and goalkeeper Jimmy Gooch, and Jackson's priority in the summer of 1955 was to reduce the average age of the squad.

He made a good start in his first season, guiding City to eighth place with one of his new players, winger Bobby Webb – an excellent free transfer signing from Leeds United – top scoring with 18 goals. Other newcomers included centre-forward Doug Kelly from Barnsley, wingers Johnny Simm from Bury, inside-forwards Les Samuels from Crewe and David Boyle from Chesterfield and defender Malcolm Currie from Scotland, as the team finished in ninth place.

More changes the following season saw City achieve their best place under Jackson – third – and while promotion continued to elude him at least City earned their place in the national Third Division in 1958 when the regional sections were scrapped and a more interesting four up four down system was introduced between Divisions Three and Four.

By this time, Jackson had signed the popular right-back Tom Flockett, who became captain, Irish centre-half Jim Lawlor and inside-forward John Reid from Scottish club Hamilton.

It was yet another player from Scotland, centre-forward John McCole, who captured the headlines the following season as he scored 28 goals, while a young Derek Stokes provided 15 goals from the left wing. City found the going tougher in the Third Division, finishing 11th, but enjoyed a good FA Cup run before going out to a last-minute goal in a fourth-round tie at Preston.

McCole was transferred to Leeds United a few weeks into the new season, but Derek Stokes switched to centre-forward and proved a more than capable deputy, scoring 25 League and a remarkable 10 goals in eight FA Cup matches as City reached the fifth round, beating First Division Everton on the way before being knocked out by future League champions Burnley after a fifth-round replay.

However, City slumped to 19th in the League, and when Stokes joined Huddersfield Town in the close season, Jackson could not replace him adequately, and as City struggled badly he was sacked the following March to bring about a sad end to what became affectionately known as the Jackson era. Two months later City were relegated to the Fourth Division.

Son David said 'Looking back, my father was more successful than most managers at Valley Parade. He had a long association with Stoke – from 1922 to 1951 as player and assistant manager, apart from two years at Southend. He was assistant manager to Bob McGrory at Stoke and played in the same team as Stanley Matthews, although he mainly looked after the second team in the Central League, the third and junior teams. He was instrumental in bringing on the post-war Stoke team that included Neil Franklin.

'He always pursued a youth policy at Wrexham and City because money wasn't available. I believe the club were in dire straits when he arrived, and he left them in good standing. His record wasn't really acknowledged. It was difficult to get promotion in those days – there were no Play-offs and no substitutes for instance, but we had a good side and we endeavoured to play good football.

'My father used Bobby Archibald, who was one of his teammates at Stoke, as Scottish scout, and he recommended some fine players to Valley Parade like John Reid, Malcolm Currie, Willie Marshall and Billy Barnes.'

Wayne Jacobs

Date of birth: 3 February 1969

Bradford City record:
Appearances: League 318, FA Cup 13, League Cup 19
Goals: League 12, FA Cup 2
Debut: 13 August 1994 v Chester City

Also played for: Sheffield Wednesday, Hull City, Rotherham United, Halifax Town
Managed: Assistant manager Halifax Town, assistant manager Bradford City

When Wayne Jacobs joined Bradford City on a free transfer in the 1994 close season, he could not have possibly imagined the sort of roller-coaster life he would experience at Valley Parade in the next 11 years. After all, City were a mid-table club in the third tier of League football when Jacobs joined them from Rotherham United, but he went on to share in two promotions and a dream appearance at Wembley. He then seized his chance to pit his skills against some of the top players in the world during two years in the Premiership, before suffering the heartache of two relegations and two financial crises that almost put the club out of business.

The ever-dependable left-back, now back at Valley Parade as assistant manager, enjoyed his Bradford City playing career, and he and his family – wife Rachel and children, Ben, Lydia and Isaac – are happily settled in the area, and he proclaims: 'I would not have traded these times for anyone'.

Sheffield-born Jacobs began his career with Sheffield Wednesday but could manage only six appearances at Hillsborough and moved to Hull City. Although he made 129 League appearances at Hull, he also suffered a bad knee injury that threatened his career. He was out of action for 12 months but then enjoyed a healing experience that brought him to Christianity, and he has since played an active part in the Christians in Sport organisation.

After a season at Rotherham United, he became one of new manager Lennie Lawrence's first signings. The club have made few better captures as Jacobs went on to make 318 League appearances and scored 12 goals before leaving on a free transfer in the summer of 2005.

Jacobs shared in City's promotion through the Play-off Final at Wembley in 1996 and the 2–0 win over Notts County and promotion to the Premiership and the memorable 3–2 win at Wolves in the dramatic last match of the 1998–99 season, followed by survival in the Premiership with a tense 1–0 win over Liverpool in another dramatic end to the season 12 months later. City survived administration in 2002 and 2004 as they suffered relegation from the top flight in 2001 and another relegation three years later.

Jacobs faced competition for the left-back position – Lee Todd, Andy Myers, Paul Heckingbottom and Bradford-born Lewis Emanuel were all competitor – but it was only in his last two seasons that he lost his regular place in the side.

He said 'I was 11 years with the club and they were fantastic times. People will say there were highs and lows – promotions and administrations, but I loved every minute of it. The biggest compliment I can give is not just to the club but that my family have settled in the area. I was born and raised in Sheffield, and I was a Sheffield Wednesday fan, but for pure commitment and the way we were made welcome I have got such an attachment to the club that Bradford City are my club now.

'The highlights of my time at Valley Parade were obviously the two promotions – to the old First Division through the Play-offs at Wembley and then to the Premiership. At one stage it seemed as if the last game of the season was such an important game – we had to win at Hull to get into the Play-offs in 1996, we had to beat Queen's Park Rangers the following year to stay up, then we had to win at Wolves in 1999 to win promotion to the Premiership, and the following year we had to beat Liverpool to stay up.

'I just look back on some amazing times and I was delighted to be part of them. It was a real blessing to my life. To play at Wembley was a dream fulfilled. What sticks out for me was the advice given by our kitman Bryan Edwards, who was a fantastic player with Bolton and won an FA Cup-winners' medal at Wembley. He told us not to let the occasion pass us by, but to enjoy the game, look around the stadium, enjoy the occasion and leave with some memories as well. What a great piece of advice from a lovely man'.

To win the game, he said, was 'a dream come true' and the final part of the day was when he and fellow Christians Andy Kiwomya, Richard Huxford went on to the pitch to pray. 'That was a special moment', he said.

'The promotion team had an affinity for each other. Everyone got on well and we were good friends. We had fantastic players – that goes without saying – and I am still in touch with more people from that era than any other. There was mutual respect and ultimately we would put ourselves on the line for each other.

'As a player it was really difficult to lose games and suffer relegations and financial crisis, but you are focussed as you go out there to play and you have to go through these things in your life and you use them to strengthen you as a person'.

Jacobs left City in 2005 after taking a testimonial, and joined Halifax Town as assistant player-manager working with his former Bradford and Rotherham teammate Chris Wilder, but was back at Valley Parade two years later as assistant manager to new manager Stuart McCall. He said 'I was really happy at Halifax, but the chance to come back was just too big. I was privileged to be asked by Stuart to join him'.

Paul Jewell

Date of birth: 28 September 1964

Bradford City record:
Appearances: League 269, FA Cup 12, League Cup 17
Goals: League 56, FA Cup 3, League 6
Debut: 27 August 1988 v Brighton & Hove Albion

Also played for: Liverpool, Wigan Athletic, Grimsby Town (loan)
Managed: Bradford City, Sheffield Wednesday, Wigan Athletic

Paul Jewell gave Bradford City 10 years' service as a player, but it is as one of the club's most successful managers that he will be best remembered by their supporters. Jewell was in charge for only two and a half years, but what a momentous period that was in the club's history as it featured two outstanding achievements – automatic promotion to the Premiership in 1998–99 followed by the minor miracle of keeping them in the top flight when the vast majority of football experts expected them to be relegated after just one season.

The only pity was that Jewell left the club to join Sheffield Wednesday in June 2000 after that first season in the Premiership. For the club declined steadily after that and found themselves back in Coca-Cola League Two – the Fourth Division – seven years later.

Jewell eased into a coaching role with City in the second half of the 1995–96 season after Chris Kamara had succeeded Lennie Lawrence as manager, and there was immediate success as the club gained promotion to the second tier of English football through the Play-offs. He continued in a coaching capacity in the following campaign as City managed to survive by beating Queen's Park Rangers in their last match, and then when Kamara was sacked midway through the next season chairman Geoffrey Richmond made Jewell caretaker manager before handing him the job on a permanent basis, when many people expected he would turn to a so-called 'big name'. It turned out to be an inspired appointment.

The club decided to make a determined promotion challenge in the 1998 close season and Jewell had some serious money to spend in the transfer market. First, he re-signed former skipper Stuart McCall from Glasgow Rangers and he then brought in three £1 million players in less than 12 months. Among them was Lee Mills from Port Vale, who repaid City's investment handsomely by scoring 23 goals in 44 League matches.

After a poor start to the season, City picked up momentum in such a spectacular way that they finished second in the table after a thrilling, never to be forgotten, 3–2 win at Wolves and won automatic promotion to the Premiership.

Most pundits expected City to go straight back down, but they survived thanks to a 1–0 win over Liverpool in a dramatic last match of the season with the goal scored by £1.4 million record signing from Leeds United David Wetherall. Jewell and his players were feted at a second civic reception in two years – the first one celebrated promotion to the Premiership 12 months earlier – but less than two months later Jewell shocked supporters by resigning to become manager of Sheffield Wednesday, later making it clear that he did not see eye to eye with Richmond and the relationship between manager and chairman had broken down.

However, he lasted less than a year at Hillsborough before he was sacked, but four months later – in the 2001 close season – he returned to his old club Wigan, in the old Second Division – the third tier of English football. This turned out to be an inspired move by Bradford-born owner Dave Whelan as Jewell guided Wigan to promotion in his second season, and two seasons later, in 2005, he led them into the Premiership. He then kept them in the top flight for two seasons before resigning soon after ensuring their survival with a dramatic win at Sheffield United in the last match of the 2006–07 season – a result that sent United down. So, Jewell has taken a break from management, but he has done so well as a manager it will be a major surprise if he doesn't come back soon.

Jewell began his playing career at his home city Liverpool as an 18-year-old, but he was unable to gain a first-team place at what was then one of the best clubs in Europe, and he was transferred to Wigan midway through the 1984–85 season. He established himself as a regular with Wigan, scoring 35 goals in 137 League appearances before Terry Dolan brought him to Valley Parade in a £80,000 deal in July 1988 as part of a rebuilding operation after City had suffered the heartache of a Second Division Play-off defeat at Middlesbrough.

Jewell formed a particularly fruitful striking partnership with Sean McCarthy after the burly forward joined City from Plymouth for £250,000 in the 1990 close season after the Bantams had been relegated from Division Two. His best season was in 1992–93, the first full season of player-manager Frank Stapleton's two and a half year spell at Valley Parade, when he scored 16 goals, while McCarthy was leading scorer with 17. He also had a good season in 1994–95 with 14 goals in 38 matches, but, after making 29 appearances – 11 of them as substitute – the following season he began to assume a coaching role at the club having scored 56 goals in 269 League appearances.

Rod Johnson

Date of birth: 8 January 1945

Bradford City record:
Appearances: League 192, FA Cup 13, League Cup 11
Goals: League 16, League Cup 3
Debut: 1 December 1973 v Colchester United

Also played for: Leeds United, Doncaster Rovers, Rotherham United, Chicago Sting, Gainsborough Trinity

Rod Johnson was a talented reserve player at Leeds during the Don Revie era in the 1960s who moved into the lower divisions to gain regular first-team football. After finding his way blocked as he tried to break into one of the most successful club sides of the post-war era, Johnson forged a successful career with three other Yorkshire sides – Doncaster Rovers, Rotherham United and Bradford City – before retiring at the age of 35 with 431 League appearances and 51 goals to his name.

Johnson, who was an England youth international, played for a Leeds Boys side that included future Leeds United teammates Paul Madeley and Paul Reaney together with future Bradford Park Avenue and Derby County ace goalscorer Kevin Hector. He joined Leeds United in 1962 after an unsuccessful trial with Reading and made his debut against Swansea that year, only to be carried off on a stretcher.

However, after making 18 League appearances in five years at Elland Road, Johnson joined Doncaster Rovers in March 1968 for £5,000, and he won a Fourth Division Championship medal in his first season. After making 107 League appearances and scoring 23 goals in just over two and half years at Doncaster, Johnson moved to South Yorkshire rivals Rotherham United in December 1970.

He made 110 League appearances in three years at Millmoor before moving to City in December 1973 in a £9,000 deal. Johnson will be remembered as a skilful midfield player, who one always felt should have played at a higher level than the Fourth Division, where he spent all but one of his six seasons at Valley Parade. However, there was a tough, hard edge to his game, which sometimes got him into trouble with referees and he was sent off twice in the 1974–75 season.

He spent the 1975 close season playing in the US with NASL club Chicago Sting before being appointed captain with City for the 1975–76 season, in which City beat Norwich City in the FA Cup – then a First Division club – before meeting Southampton at home in the quarter-final. It was the first time that City had reached the last eight of the FA Cup for 56 years, but the result was a disappointment as they lost 1–0 to the eventual winners of the trophy.

Johnson remembers the Southampton game as a highlight of his time at Valley Parade. 'They seemed destined to win the Cup, but we were unlucky and the Southampton manager, Lawrie McMenemy, who had been my manager at Doncaster, agreed. He said Southampton were fortunate to win that day.'

Johnson missed only two League matches that season and played in all six FA Cup matches, and the following season he had the satisfaction of captaining the side that won promotion to the Third Division, making 40 League appearances. Unfortunately, injury restricted his appearances to only 20 the following season as City failed to hold on to their newly found Third Division place and slipped back to Division Four. In fact, he missed the first half of a season where City badly needed his experience and leadership.

Johnson was given some coaching duties, but after making 26 League appearances back in the Fourth Division he was released at the end of the 1978–79 season having played 192 League matches and made 24 Cup appearances.

'I have no regrets at any of my career and I enjoyed my time at Bradford,' he said. 'You cannot look back. I never enjoyed myself at Rotherham, but I enjoyed it at Leeds and Bradford and we won the Championship at Doncaster.'

After his release by City, Johnson joined non-League Gainsborough Trinity after turning down Doncaster and Crewe, but didn't last long at Gainsborough as he left to concentrate on his new job with Pearl Insurance.

Nowadays he works in the service department of Mercedes Benz at Leeds while selling properties aboard with his son Simon. And there may be another footballer in the family as his grandson Jack is at the Leeds United Academy.

Chris Kamara

Date of birth: 25 December 1957

Bradford City record:
Appearances: League 23, FA Cup 2, League Cup 3
Goals: League 3
Debut: 13 August 1994 v Chester City

Also played for: Portsmouth (twice), Swindon Town (twice), Brentford, Stoke City, Leeds United, Luton Town, Sheffield United (loan), Middlesbrough (loan)
Managed: Bradford City, Stoke City

Chris Kamara gave Bradford City supporters something most of them could only dream about – a day out at Wembley, twin towers and all. At one time, of course, the only way a club could go to Wembley was by way of the FA Cup – and later the Football League Cup. However, the Play-offs changed all that, but the sight of City running out on the hallowed at Wembley was still a wonderful sight for those 30,000 travelling fans on that memorable day in May 1996.

And the day had a happy ending when City beat Notts County 2–0 in the Second Division Play-off Final to return to Division One – by then the second tier of English football – after a gap of six years.

Kamara joined City as a player in the 1994 close season, one of Lennie Lawrence's signings after he replaced Frank Stapleton as manager, but it is as a manager that he will be remembered by all at Valley Parade.

He made 23 League appearances in his first season to bring his tally to an impressive 641 and 73 goals in a career that began as an apprentice at Portsmouth and took in two spells at Swindon and a second spell at Portsmouth, Brentford, Stoke City, Leeds United, Luton Town, two spells at Sheffield United, Middlesbrough and finally Bradford City.

Lawrence promoted him to be assistant manager in 1995, and when the club decided to sack Lawrence at the end of November chairman Geoffrey Richmond decided to appoint Kamara in his place. The early stages of Kamara's managerial career didn't go well, and at the end of February a Play-off place looked to be a distant prospect, but City lost only four of their last 16 matches to make sure of sixth place with a thrilling 3–2 win at Hull City in the final game of the season.

They then beat Blackpool in a memorable Play-off semi-final, coming back from a 2–0 defeat in the first leg at Valley Parade to win 3–0 at Bloomfield Road and get through 3–2 on aggregate to set up a Final against Notts County at Wembley. Fortunately for City, local boy Des Hamilton settled everyone's nerves with a goal after seven minutes, and Mark Stallard, whom Kamara had signed from Derby County just over a month after he had taken over as manager, made sure of promotion with a second goal 16 minutes from the end to spark a round of celebrations that included a civic reception in Bradford the following day.

However, staying in the higher division proved to be difficult and City did not secure their First Division future until the last match of the season.

With little or no money to spend in the transfer market because the club were still paying for the new £1.5 million Midland Road stand, Kamara was forced to concentrate on free transfers under the Bosman Ruling in the first half of the season. The result was a procession of foreign players coming into Valley Parade – some of them successful, others less so – but one player who captured everyone's imagination was the former England international winger, Chris Waddle, who delighted fans for five months before leaving for Sunderland. Kamara also signed Middlesbrough goalkeeper Mark Schwarzer from German club Kaiserslautern and sold him four months later for £1.3 million.

Meanwhile, after an eventful season of comings and goings, Kamara's team were left needing to win their last two matches – both at Valley Parade – to ensure their survival, and they beat Charlton 1–0 on General Election day before beating Queen's Park Rangers 3–0 on the final day of the season.

Kamara planned for the new season with a string of good signings like Robbie Blake – signed six weeks before the old season ended – Peter Beagrie, Jamie Lawrence and Darren Moore, but one who was not so good was Bolton striker John McGinlay, who was bought for £625,000. 'The following season we were short of goals and needed to sign a goalscorer. I thought McGinlay was the man. I had seen him scoring goals for Bolton, but he didn't do himself justice at Bradford City. We checked him out medically and he seemed fine, but in my final game – a third-round FA Cup tie at Manchester City – he missed three wonderful chances.'

City lost 2–0 and three days later Kamara was sacked, but he said 'I had no hint that the sacking was coming. I thought I was unsackable. Sackings happen in football. Mine was nonsense. If I had done something wrong or I was struggling, I would have held my hands up and said "OK." But the club was moving forward. We were heading for the Premiership, that was our aim. I still believe we would have made the Play-offs that season.

Kamara was keen to stay in management and quickly took the manager's job at his old club Stoke, but they were having a bad run, and he admitted 'I was in the right place at the wrong time', and he negotiated his release before the end of the season.

He went into media work in television, radio and newspapers and is a high-profile football commentator on Sky TV.

Jim Lawlor

Date of birth: 10 May 1933

Bradford City record:
Appearances: League 153, FA Cup 20, League Cup 3
Goals: League 5, FA Cup 2
Debut: 3 April 1957 v Derby County

Also played for: Transport FC, Shamrock Rovers, Doncaster Rovers, Coleraine

Irishman Jim Lawlor was a Bradford City regular centre-half for six seasons in the late 1950s and early 1960s before a broken leg in May 1962 cruelly ended his career. Lawlor recalls 'I was playing in a reserve match at Sunderland when I broke my leg. It was the last match of the season. I was left with one leg slightly shorter than the other so that was the end of my career. Some people get caps and medals – I got a broken leg. It happened when I was at my peak. I was only 28. You only begin to know the game when you have been around a bit.'

Born at Finglas Bridge near Dublin, Lawlor joined Shamrock Rovers from Transport FC before coming to England to try his luck as a professional with Doncaster Rovers, where his brother John also played. Unfortunately, he had to wait for two years before making his League debut, and after making only 10 League appearances he returned to Ireland in the 1955 close season to sign for Coleraine, and the following September he represented the Irish League against the Scottish League.

He decided to come back to England and joined City in March 1957. He immediately gained a regular place, playing in the club's last nine matches of that season. He said 'I enjoyed my time at Valley Parade. There was a great atmosphere in the place. We had a good group of players and we all played for each other. We got on very well together. You enjoyed the people you played with in matches and in training. That was the good thing about our era in the game. We got little or nothing from it, but we enjoyed it.'

Lawlor remembers the 2-0 win in the FA Cup third round at Brighton in January 1959 as one of the best performances of his time at Valley Parade. City lost goalkeeper Geoff Smith in the first minute – there were no substitutes in those days – and centre-forward John McCole went in goal, but goals from David Jackson and Derek Stokes enabled City to earn a fourth-round tie at Preston. 'Brighton were a decent side in the Second Division,' said Lawlor, 'but we beat them soundly 2-0.'

After going down 2-0 at half-time against Preston, City hit back to level the scores at 2-2 with goals from McCole and Lawlor, only to go out of the Cup to a late goal. Lawlor recalls 'Preston were in the First Division at the time, and they have some very good players, although their most famous player Tom Finney did not play in this match. We were going well at 2-2 after coming back from 2-0 down when we let in a late goal.'

There was more Cup drama the following season when City reached the fifth round, only to crash out 5-0 in a replay at First Division Burnley after the teams had drawn 2-2 at Valley Parade, but City nearly didn't reach the second round. Lawlor recalls that City trailed 3-1 at Barnsley in the first round, only to fight back to level the scores at 3-3 and then win the replay at Valley Parade 2-1.

City then beat Rochdale in the second round after a replay to set up a third-round tie against First Division Everton in front of a 23,550 crowd at Valley Parade. Two divisions separated the teams, but Lawlor recalls 'We had a thumping 3-0 win. Everton had internationals in their side like centre-half Brian Labone, inside-forward Bobby Collins, who later played for Leeds United, and right-back Alex Parker. We played David Boyle as a makeshift left-winger, but he was a natural right-sided player and he always cut in on his right foot and Parker couldn't make head or tail of him.'

City beat Bournemouth in the next round to set up the Burnley tie. They went into a 2-0 lead against Burnley in front of a 26,227 capacity crowd at Valley Parade, only to concede two late goals before crashing out of the Cup in the replay, with 52,850 crowding into Turf Moor. 'Burnley had eight or nine internationals in their team, but it was the two wingers, John Connelly and Brian Pilkington, who did the damage. I heard that Jimmy McIlroy wasn't impressed with our muddy pitch. He was lucky – he didn't have to play on it every week,' he said.

Lawlor, who was granted a benefit match one month before he broke his leg, made 153 League appearances for City and scored five goals. He also played in 23 Cup matches with two goals. Lawlor left Valley Parade in February 1963 but returned in June 1964 as a full-time pools agent, and when manager Bob Brocklebank left the following October, after City made a bad start to the season, he doubled up as reserve-team trainer.

In fact, he took charge of the first team for two matches in the November when City gained a surprise 1-0 win at Charlton in the League Cup and also when they beat Newport County at home in the League three days later – former City favourite John McCole was in the visitors' side that day. Another member of the backroom staff, Ted Broughton, also took charge for a few matches before City eventually recruited Welsh international Bill Harris from Middlesbrough as player-manager the following March.

Lawlor left City again in 1965 and spent nine years as a pools promoter with Bramley Rugby League Club before becoming development manager at Bradford Northern RLFC. He became an active member of the Bradford City and Park Avenue Ex-Players' Association, looking after the welfare of needy ex-players.

Jamie Lawrence

Date of birth: 8 March 1970

Bradford City record:
Appearances: League 155, FA Cup 5, League 9
Goals: League 12, FA Cup 5, League Cup 9
Debut: 9 August 1997 v Stockport County

Also played for: Sunderland, Doncaster Rovers, Leicester City, Walsall, Wigan Athletic, Grimsby Town, Brentford, Fisher Athletic

No one could ignore Jamie Lawrence. With his pineapple shaped barnet and his hair of many colours, Jamie was the centre of attention even before he began to play. Fans loved him because although he enjoyed an extrovert lifestyle he never failed to give of his best. The various other escapades, including some criminal adventures, that make up his colourful personality are graphically described in his aptly named autobiography *From Prison to the Premiership*.

However, despite his playboy image, Lawrence was a serious footballer, who made 155 League appearances in six seasons at Valley Parade and was a key member of the Bradford City team that won promotion to the Premiership and kept them there.

A competitive right-sided midfield player who could also operate as a traditional winger, Lawrence liked to run with the ball and deliver telling crosses, but was also strong in the tackle. He joined City in the summer of 1997 from Leicester City for a bargain £50,000, one of several key signings made by manager Chris Kamara to strengthen a team that had narrowly escaped relegation from the old First Division when it was the second tier of English football. Others included Peter Beagrie, Gary Walsh and Darren Moore. Little could Lawrence have realised that two years later he would be celebrating promotion to the Premiership.

That Lawrence should play professional football at all was a minor miracle considering his turbulent early life. Born in south London of West Indian parents as part of a large family, Lawrence had a tough life. He was a promising footballer at school, but after his parents returned to Jamaica when he was 17 Lawrence fell into a life of petty crime and twice went to prison. It was during his second spell in prison at Camp Hill on the Isle of Wight that he not only began to turn his life around, but he made an impression as a potential League footballer.

Initially he played for the prison team, but he was so good that he was allowed out of prison every week to play for a local side, Cowes Sports, in the Hampshire League. This unusual arrangement naturally attracted attention from local television and newspapers and the prison authorities were keen to parade Jamie as a good example of their rehabilitation programme. Scouts from Southampton, Portsmouth and Watford were among the clubs who came to watch him, and when he left Camp Hill in 1993 aged 23 he had trials with Southend, Millwall and Wimbledon before signing for Sunderland under former England defender Terry Butcher.

Lawrence made only four League appearances for Sunderland before he joined Doncaster Rovers later that season, and after 10 months there, during which time he played in 25 League matches, he got his big break – a £125,000 move to the Premiership with Leicester City – the first signing for manager Mark McGhee. Unfortunately, Leicester were relegated that season, and when McGhee left to join Wolves he was replaced by current Aston Villa and former Celtic manager Martin O'Neill.

He guided them to promotion through the Play-offs in his first season and Leicester won the Coca-Cola Cup in O'Neill's second season, beating Middlesbrough in the Final after a replay. Lawrence didn't play in the first match but came on as substitute for the last 20 minutes of the replay, when a last-minute goal scored by former Bradford City striker Steve Claridge sealed the win. They also finished 10th in the Premiership, but although O'Neill offered Lawrence a one-year contract he told him he couldn't guarantee him a first-team place, so the player agreed to leave and City signed him.

Lawrence rarely enjoyed a regular first-team place at Leicester, making just 47 League appearances in two and a half years, 26 of them as substitute, but in his first season at Valley Parade he made 43 League appearances, only five of them as a substitute.

Kamara was sacked midway through the season and replaced by his number two Paul Jewell, and Lawrence played a key part in the team that Jewell put together that would lift City into the Premiership.

Lawrence's form for City earned him international selection for Jamaica in the summer of 2000, and he played 42 games for his country over four years, including World Cup qualifiers. Playing against world class players improved his game. He began to pass the ball better and took his place in central-midfield for City.

Lawrence was troubled by injury in his last three seasons, breaking an arm, a leg and having a groin operation, and never played more than half the League matches, making 17 appearances in 2000–01, the last in the Premiership, 21 in 2001–02 and 16 in his last season. He left City on transfer deadline day 2003 to join Walsall.

Besides Walsall, Lawrence has also played for Wigan on loan under Paul Jewell, Grimsby, where Nicky Law signed him, and Brentford since leaving Valley Parade. He now works back in south London as a player and fitness coach for Rymans League club Fisher Athletic and has ambitions to get all his coaching qualifications, so he can coach or manage at the top level.

David Layne

Date of birth: 29 July 1939

Bradford City record:
Appearances: League 65, FA Cup 3, League Cup 1
Goals: League 44, FA Cup 2, League Cup 1
Debut: 26 December 1960 v Hull City

Also played for: Rotherham United, Swindon Town, Sheffield Wednesday, Hereford United

David Layne played only 18 months at Bradford City, but it was long enough for him to write his name into the club record books. Bronco, as he was known, was one of Peter Jackson's signings, but the manager did not stay long enough at Valley Parade to reap the benefit of the centre-forward's lethal striking rate. For, in 65 League matches, Layne scored 44 goals, including a record 34 in his first full season – a record that still stands. He was a strong, bustling type of centre-forward with a hard shot.

Layne was born at Sheffield and began his career as a part-time player with Rotherham United. Unfortunately, he could not gain a regular place at Millmoor, and after scoring four goals in 11 matches he joined Swindon Town on a free transfer. It was at Swindon that he first showed his prolific goalscoring form, and after scoring a remarkable 28 goals in 41 games City signed him for £6,000 in December 1960 as a 21-year-old, breaking their 40-year-old transfer record, and he made his debut at home to Hull City on Boxing Day.

The background to the signing was that City had sold their goalscoring centre-forward Derek Stokes to Huddersfield Town the previous summer and had not replaced him. Consequently, they were struggling for goals, and even by December they were in danger of relegation, having won only five matches by the halfway mark. Jackson paid the price for this poor form when he was sacked in the March, but his dismissal made no difference to the season's outcome, and City were relegated to the Fourth Division for the first time.

Layne did well, scoring 10 goals in 22 matches, but he did even better the following season when City made a bold bid to win promotion back to the Third Division at the first attempt under new manager Bob Brocklebank, who had previously managed Chesterfield, Birmingham City and Hull City. At the halfway mark in the season, City had won only six matches and a promotion challenge looked to be out of the question, especially when over the Christmas period they suffered their record defeat – a 9-1 humiliation at Colchester four days after beating them 4-1 at Valley Parade. The season was further disrupted in the January when Bradford suffered the effects of a smallpox outbreak.

However, City made a significant signing in the October when former centre-forward John McCole rejoined them from Leeds United and struck up a useful partnership with Layne, his skill providing a string of chances that Bronco gratefully accepted. Nonetheless, City were in urgent need of a revival and it started with a 2-0 win at Accrington Stanley on 3 February. In fact, City won seven matches in a row, scoring 23 goals in the process, but a fortnight after beating Accrington the club went out of business and all points gained against them were deleted from the records – a decision that would ultimately cost them promotion.

City ended the season strongly, winning 14 and losing only two of their last 18 matches, and Layne ended it with a flourish as he scored 11 of City's 21 goals in their last seven matches. Crucially, though, they lost the penultimate match of the season 5-3 at Workington, and although they beat Wrexham by the same score at home in the final fixture it was not enough to win promotion and they finished in fifth place, frustratingly one place outside the promotion places.

Layne's record 34 goals included three hat-tricks – against Crewe and Gillingham at home and Carlisle away – and having failed to gain promotion there was no way the club could keep him. As soon as the season was over he moved back to his home city, joining First Division Sheffield Wednesday for a club record £22,500.

The big question was could Layne continue his goalscoring form in the top division. The answer was yes, and he finished the next two seasons at Hillsborough as top scorer, netting a remarkable 52 goals in 74 matches, but then his career came to a sad halt. Layne was one of the players found guilty of taking part in the infamous soccer bribes scandal of the early 1960s, involving match rigging and a betting coup. He was jailed for three months and banned for life. The FA lifted the ban, and he rejoined Wednesday in 1972 but could not recapture his earlier form and went on loan to Hereford United. After only four League matches for Hereford, he moved to non-League Matlock Town until injury forced him to retire from the game, leaving him with the enviable record of 128 goals from only 195 League matches and the rest of us wondering just what this remarkable player could have achieved had he not been banned.

Ken Leek

Date of birth: 26 July 1935

Bradford City record:
Appearances: League 99, FA Cup 2, League Cup 3
Goals: League 25, League Cup 1
Debut: 6 November 1965 v Doncaster Rovers

Also played for: Northampton Town (twice), Leicester City, Newcastle United, Birmingham City, Rhyl Athletic
Managed: Rhyl Athletic (player-coach)

Welsh international Ken Leek made history when he became City's record £10,000 signing. Stafford Heginbotham was determined to make a splash when he took over as chairman in October 1965 with his friend David Ide and immediately made money available for signings.

City were busy in the transfer market in the weeks after Heginbotham's arrival, but it was the signing of 30-year-old Leek that made the most impact with the Bradford public. The team needed a goalscorer and to sign a player of Leek's pedigree was an exciting development for City who had made a miserable start to their Fourth Division season with a mere two wins and 10 defeats in their first 14 matches.

Leek never turned out to be the goalscorer that City needed, and although he was top scorer with 11 goals in 24 League appearances in his first season in his favoured centre-forward role he could not prevent them from having to seek re-election. From then on, he gradually reverted to a midfield role where his strength, skill and experience made him a valuable if not quite dominant figure.

He scored 26 goals in 104 League and Cup appearances in three seasons before leaving Valley Parade in June 1968 to join Rhyl Athletic as player-coach. He also played for other Welsh sides, Merthyr Tydfil and Ton Pentre before retiring.

Four years before joining City, Leek had captured national headlines when Leicester City surprisingly dropped him on the eve of the 1961 FA Cup Final, despite the fact that he had been instrumental in taking them to Wembley by scoring in every round on their way to the Final. It was a move that shook the football world and had a shattering effect on Leek, which was a shame because he enjoyed a proud record of averaging just over one goal in every three League and Cup matches for Leicester. Moving into the First Division with Leicester from Fourth Division Northampton was a big move for the Welshman. He joined them initially as an inside or outside-left, but was soon competing for the number-nine shirt and gained his first six full Welsh caps while he was at the club.

Inevitably, he decided to leave Leicester in the summer of 1961 after the Cup Final blow, having scored 43 goals in 111 League and Cup appearances in three years, and after a brief spell with Newcastle he moved back to the Midlands with Birmingham City in November 1961. During a three-year spell at St Andrew's, Leek continued his consistent goalscoring record, the highlight being the two goals he scored to help the Blues to victory over local rivals Aston Villa in the 1963 League Cup Final.

Leek began his Football League career with Northampton Town in April 1958 and it was to there that he returned in December 1964, after three years at Birmingham, but less than a year later he was on the move again, this time to Valley Parade.

It was while he was at Northampton the first time around that Leek first gained international honours when he was capped at Under-23 level for his country, and he went on to win 17 full Welsh caps. By the time he returned to finish his career in his native Wales, Leek had scored 147 League goals.

He later settled back in Northamptonshire in the Daventry area, working for Ford Motors.

Peter Logan

Date of birth: 1889
Died: 1944

Bradford City record:
Appearances: League 271, FA Cup 33
Goals: League 37, FA Cup 6
Debut: 24 October 1908 v Sunderland

Also played for: Alvan Rangers, Edinburgh St Bernards

Scot Peter Logan was at the heart of some of the most momentous events in City's chequered history and became an popular figure at Valley Parade in his 17 seasons at the club. Born at Edinburgh, Logan joined City in October 1908 after playing for Alva Rangers and the famous Scottish junior club Edinburgh St Bernard's just two months into the club's first season in the First Division, following in the footsteps of his brother James who had been on the books from April 1905 to August 1906.

During his long spell at Valley Parade, he filled every position in the forward line except centre-forward and made 304 League and Cup appearances, scoring 43 goals.

Undoubtedly the highlight of his career was season 1910-11 when City not only achieved their highest ever League placing but won the FA Cup, beating Newcastle United 1-0 in a replay at Old Trafford after the first match at Crystal Palace had ended in a 0-0 draw. Logan played in all seven matches during that momentous Cup campaign, four of them on the right wing when Dickie Bond was suspended. He also wore the number-seven shirt in the two final matches and was one of eight Scotsmen in the Cup-winning side.

Logan made his debut at home to Sunderland in October 1908, but made only seven appearances in that first season as City survived in the top flight only by winning their last match at home to Manchester City. The following season he established himself as a regular player on the left wing, with 29 League and Cup appearances, and he played on both flanks the following season as City achieved their highest ever placing – fifth in the top flight – and won the FA Cup, although he lost his place on the left wing in the second half of the season after manager Peter O'Rourke signed Irish international Frank Thompson.

Those were the days of set positions in football – the game was tactically less fluid than it is today when teams adopt a variety of formations – but Logan was nothing if not versatile and made the most of 34 League and Cup appearances the following season at inside-right.

However, he clearly had a preference for the left wing, and he played most of his matches

there as he continued to make a significant contribution to City until League football was suspended in 1915 because of the war. He played 67 wartime matches for City while serving in the army, winning representative honours for his army unit, and when League football resumed in 1919 he was the club's longest-serving player.

Logan made 76 League appearances in City's last three seasons in the First Division, including 30 in 1921-22 when City lost their top flight status. His commitment to the City cause continued after they were relegated to the Second Division, and he played for three more seasons until he retired in 1925 with 271 League appearances and 37 goals.

Logan became club coach after he retired, but he left in October 1925 to become licensee of the Girlington Hotel in Bradford. He died in Bradford in 1944, aged 54.

Stuart McCall

Date of birth: 10 June 1964

Bradford City record:
Appearances: League 395, FA Cup 17, League Cup 27
Goals: League 45, FA Cup 3, League Cup 4
Debut: 28 August 1982 v Reading

Also played for: Everton, Glasgow Rangers, Sheffield United
Managed: Assistant manager Sheffield United, manager Bradford City

Stuart McCall is easily the most popular Bradford City player of the post-war era. What more could a manager want from a midfield player – or of any player for that matter? McCall was enthusiastic, committed, hard working and loyal, a player who led by example, who never gave less than 100 percent, someone who could tackle and pass the ball and, above all, he has an exemplary attitude. Off the field, he was also a player who would work in the community and enjoyed a special rapport with children and young people.

When McCall joined City as an apprentice in 1980, he was a slightly-built 16-year-old who had been playing for Farsley Celtic's junior team. He made an immediate impression on everyone at Valley Parade, but it was two years before he made his League debut – at right-back in August 1982 in a 3-2 home win over Reading. It was City's first season back in the Third Division after winning promotion, and before the end of the campaign he had slotted into his familiar midfield role wearing his famous number-four shirt.

McCall played a key role in the club's Third Division Championship triumph in 1985 – one of two ever presents – and when Peter Jackson left to go to Newcastle United in October 1986 he took over the captaincy. However, it became certain sooner rather than later that McCall would want to test his ability at the top level – if not with Bradford City then with another club. He and City's other star player, John Hendrie, might have left in the 1987 close season, but they agreed to stay another season to help them reach the top flight. They almost made it, but lost out on an automatic promotion place by losing to Ipswich on the final day of the 1987–88 season; they were then beaten in the Second Division Play-offs by Middlesbrough.

McCall describes City's Third Division Championship season as a 'brilliant time'. 'There was a massive belief, and we started emerging as a team; I think football lifted the City as well. It was brilliant to be associated with Bradford.' However, following City's failure to gain promotion, McCall fulfilled his ambition to play in the top flight when he joined Everton in a £850,000 deal, and he scored two goals as they won the FA Cup in his first season. Just over two years later, he made another big move - to Glasgow Rangers – and won a string of Cups and League Championships in his seven years at Ibrox, along with 40 Scotland caps.

His return to Valley Parade in the summer of 1998 was a surprise to City supporters. He still had a year to run on his Rangers contract, but all the players who had been associated with manager Walter Smith were leaving, and Rangers allowed him to leave on a free transfer provided he joined an English club. So, he signed for City, was appointed captain and helped them to reach the promised land of the Premiership in his memorable first season.

McCall was appointed assistant manager to Chris Hutchings when Paul Jewell left a month after City's dramatic Premiership survival. He was also caretaker manager for a couple of matches after Hutchins was sacked following a bad start to the season, before former Hearts manager Jim Jefferies took over.

McCall left City in May 2002, at the end of his four-year contract, to join Sheffield United as a player with coaching responsibilities and played two seasons before retiring at the age of 40 to bring his superb 24-year career to an end. He became assistant manager at Bramall Lane and helped manager Neil Warnock to guide the Blades into the Premiership in the 2005–06 season. However, they were relegated 12 months later, Warnock resigned, and when United decided not to make McCall manager he – City's number-one target to succeed Colin Todd – came back to Valley Parade as boss.

So, now he has the task of restoring the club's fortunes after three relegations in six years. He said 'It was an emotional decision and one led massively by my heart. I made the decision that the 2006–07 season would be my last as a number two. I had one year in the Premiership and it was time to move on. I was ready to become a manager and deep down in my subconscious I always wanted to come back to Bradford. If I'm going to be successful as a manager then I want it to be with Bradford City. I haven't got a magic wand, but what the fans are guaranteed is that they will get total commitment both on and off the field.

Sean McCarthy

Date of birth: 12 September 1967

Bradford City record:
Appearances: League 131, FA Cup 8, League Cup 12
Goals: League 60, FA Cup 2, League Cup 10
Debut: 25 August 1990 v Tranmere Rovers

Also played for: Swansea City, Plymouth Argyle (twice), Oldham Athletic, Bristol City, Exeter City

To average one goal in every two matches is the dream of every striker and that is the superb strike rate that Sean McCarthy achieved in three and a half seasons at Valley Parade. Having failed to keep City in the Second Division in his first two months – the side were in a precarious position when he took over from Terry Yorath in March 1990 – new manager John Docherty looked to solve the team's chronic goalscoring problems with a player who had a good track record at Third Division level.

So, he splashed out £250,000 on Plymouth striker Sean McCarthy. Although City failed to make progress during his spell at the club, that was not the fault of McCarthy, who scored 60 goals in 131 League matches – an impressive record by any standards – and was leading scorer in each of his four seasons at Valley Parade.

McCarthy was not the most hard working of players, but he came alive in the penalty area where his strong, sturdy build not only enabled him to score goals himself, but create chances for other players. One player to benefit was his striking partner Paul Jewell, and they formed an effective partnership during his spell at Valley Parade while becoming firm friends off the field. Their best season together was in 1992-93 when they scored 33 goals between them – 17 for McCarthy and 16 for Jewell.

McCarthy made an explosive start to the 1993-94 season with 14 League goals in the first 18 matches and seven in the League Cup, as City thrashed Darlington 11-1 in a two-leg tie. Not surprisingly, this sort of strike rate began to attract the attention of bigger clubs, and the club needed to sell to ease their difficult financial position. Although it was inevitable that City would be forced to offload their most saleable asset, it was nonetheless frustrating for supporters to see their leading goalscorer having to leave Valley Parade.

McCarthy had scored a late equaliser for City at Cardiff on the last Saturday in November 1993, but before they faced an FA Cup replay at Chester four days later, a deal had been arranged to take the striker to Oldham Athletic, then managed by Joe Royle. The £500,000 deal involved young striker Neil Tolson coming to Valley Parade. It was later revealed that City had received only £350,000 from the deal, which clearly over valued Tolson, who didn't measure up as an adequate replacement for McCarthy. The truth was that City were desperate to sell to pay an urgent debt. So they were in a weak position when negotiating with Oldham and didn't receive as much for McCarthy as they hoped to do.

It says a lot about the rest of the team that even though McCarthy left City at the end of November he still ended the season as leading scorer with 14 League goals in 18 matches and seven in the League Cup.

McCarthy spent three and a half years at Oldham, averaging almost one goal in every three matches as he scored 42 goals in 140 League games before he had a brief spell at Bristol City. He returned to Plymouth in 1998 before ending his League career at their West Country rivals Exeter City in 2001.

After a spell as a part-time coach at Plymouth, he now runs the Football in the Community Programme at Premiership side Portsmouth.

'I enjoyed my time at Bradford,' he said. 'It was a successful spell in my career to score roughly one goal in every two matches. I had a good partnership with Paul Jewell which resulted in a strong friendship and we still keep in touch.'

John McCole

Date of birth: 18 September 1936
Died: 1981

Bradford City record:
Appearances: League 88, FA Cup 9, League Cup 2
Goals: League 47, FA Cup 7, League Cup 1
Debut: 20 September 1958 v Southampton

Also played for: Falkirk, Leeds United, Rotherham United, Newport County, Shelbourne

There have been few more talented footballers at Valley Parade in the post-war era than Scottish centre-forward John McCole. The sad aspect from Bradford City's point of view is that his two spells at Valley Parade were all too brief.

McCole joined City from Falkirk in September 1958 and the story is that the club's trainer Jock Robertson gave him special training to enable him to cope with extra pace of the English game. The training must have worked as McCole enjoyed a superb first season combining skill, an astute football brain and lethal finishing as he broke the club's scoring record with 28 goals in 34 League matches plus six in four FA Cup ties.

McCole scored on his debut as City went down 3-2 to Southampton at Valley Parade and went on to score no fewer than three hat-tricks – in a 7-1 home win over Rochdale and a 6-1 win at home to Southend in the League and in a 4-3 victory in an FA Cup first-round tie at Mansfield. He also scored both goals in City's 2-0 win at Bradford Park Avenue in the FA Cup second round and ended the season with a flourish, scoring 12 goals in the last nine matches.

At the same time, Derek Stokes scored 15 goals in 45 appearances plus one in the Cup from the left wing. Despite these goalscoring feats, City could still only finish in 11th place.

McCole continued where he had left off when the new season began, scoring four goals in the first eight matches when he was suddenly transferred to Leeds United with the campaign less than a month old. Nothing was made public at the time, but it is understood he had a fall out with manager Peter Jackson and within days he was sold to City's West Yorkshire neighbours for a £10,000 fee.

It seemed to be a giveaway fee even by the values of those days, especially when McCole continued his goalscoring exploits for Leeds in the First Division, but initially City did not seem to suffer as Jackson successfully switched Stokes from the left wing to centre-forward, and he scored 35 League and Cup goals as the club reached the FA Cup fifth round.

McCole was an instant success at Elland Road, scoring six goals in his first eight matches, and was leading scorer with an impressive 22 that season. Unfortunately for Leeds, they had a leaky defence and were relegated after four years in the top flight. The team included Don Revie, who was soon to transform Leeds into one of the best teams in the country, leading them to League Championship and Cup triumphs during his 10 years as manager. Also playing alongside McCole that season were Jack Charlton, who managed the Republic of Ireland after 20 years at Elland Road, future City manager Grenville Hair, who tragically died during a training session at Valley Parade in 1968, future City midfield player Peter McConnell, while Billy Bremner also made his debut.

McCole scored an impressive 45 goals in 78 League appearances during his two years at Leeds, as well as eight Cup goals, including four goals in a League Cup tie at Brentford in September 1961.

Just as McCole's departure from Valley Parade was a surprise, so was his return in October 1961 under new manager Bob Brocklebank. After City had won only four of their first 16 matches, supporters welcomed McCole's return, but he played a different role from his first spell. City had signed a new centre-forward, David Layne, the season before, and Brocklebank gave McCole a free role, usually on the left, where he used his skill and vision as a playmaker.

It was partly thanks to the openings that he provided that Layne was able to break McCole's own scoring record of 28 League goals set three years earlier, while McCole himself scored 10 goals.

Layne left for Sheffield Wednesday during the summer after City just missed out on promotion, and McCole resumed his centre-forward role the following season, but he was on the move again in the December when he joined Rotherham.

Unfortunately, McCole's career went downhill from there. He broke his leg the following year and was out of action for a year. After making a mere 14 appearances with Rotherham, McCole had a short spell in Ireland with Shelbourne, but he returned to the English League in October 1964 with Newport County. There, he had the misfortune to break his leg twice, and after playing only six matches with Newport he went back to Ireland in February 1965 to play with Cork Hibernians. Sadly he died in Ireland in 1981, aged only 45.

McCole played 186 League matches in England, scoring an impressive 99 goals, including 47 goals in 88 League matches for City, for whom he also scored eight Cup goals. What a pity he didn't make more of his ability.

Jimmy McDonald

Date of birth: 1885

Bradford City record:
Appearances: League 202, FA Cup 25
Goals: League 25, FA Cup 1
Debut: 20 April 1907 v Burton United

Also played for: Edinburgh St Bernards, Raith Rovers

Jimmy McDonald

Jimmy McDonald, seated on the ground on the left, in the 1907–08 team photograph.

Scot Jimmy McDonald was one of City's most influential players before World War One as the club won promotion to the First Division and established themselves in the top flight. A skilful, ball-winning midfield player – he began at inside-forward and later played at left-half – McDonald joined City from the famous Scottish junior club, Edinburgh St Bernard's, from where they also signed Peter Logan two years later in April 1907 – the same month that fellow Scot, centre-forward Frank O'Rourke, also joined them from Airdrieonians – and made a good early impression, scoring on his debut – a 3-2 home defeat against Burton United.

Manager Peter O'Rourke clearly saw Frank O'Rourke and McDonald as key signings to take the club forward, and the two players struck up a fine understanding in their first full season as City won the Second Division title. In fact, that turned out to be McDonald's best season with City as he missed only two League matches and scored 13 goals in 36 League appearances.

He made only 24 League appearances over the next two seasons, as City established themselves in Division One, but played a full part in the FA Cup-winning team despite being involved in a late night escapade in Otley with teammates Dickie Bond and Robert Campbell. Peter O'Rourke threatened to suspend all three players sine die, but they were reinstated a few weeks later, and although McDonald missed the first-round tie at New Brompton – now Gillingham – he played in the remaining six matches, including the final against Newcastle United at the Crystal Palace and the replay at Old Trafford, which City won 1-0.

At the same time, McDonald also played 18 League matches as City achieved their highest-ever placing – fifth in the top division.

McDonald regained a regular place in the seasons leading up to the war, as City became a good class Division One side, and became such an influential player that he was appointed captain. In fact, he made 118 League appearances in four seasons before League football was suspended in 1915. He was a military driver during the war and made 42 wartime appearances while playing for his unit in charity games.

By the time League football resumed after the war, McDonald was in his mid-30s, and he made only three appearances in 1919-20 before deciding to return to Scotland and play for Raith Rovers.

Roy McFarland

Date of birth: 5 April 1948

Bradford City record:
Appearances: League 40, FA Cup 2, League Cup 4
Goals: League 1
Debut: 19 August 1981 v Wigan Athletic

Also played for: Tranmere Rovers, Derby County
Managed: Bradford City, Bolton Wanderers, Cambridge United, Torquay United, Chesterfield

Former England defender Roy McFarland spent only 18 months at Valley Parade, but it proved to be an influential period. Some people will choose to remember only his controversial departure in November 1982 when he returned to Derby County. The club were later found guilty of poaching him to join a new managerial team and were ordered to pay £55,000 in compensation, while McFarland was banned from playing – a ban that was lifted nine months later.

However, City supporters would be wise to celebrate McFarland's inspirational leadership on and off the field as the club gained promotion from the old Fourth Division. That promotion laid the foundations for an even greater success three years later, when his successor – another former England defender – Trevor Cherry led them to the Third Division Championship.

McFarland began his playing career at Tranmere Rovers and the story is that Brain Clough got him out of bed one night in August 1967 to persuade him to sign for Derby. It turned out to be a great move for both club and player. McFarland was one of Clough's first signings as he set about building a great side that would win the Second Division Championship in his first season, two League Championships and reach the European Cup semi-finals.

At the same time the player went on to gain 28 England caps and would have gained many more had his career not been plagued by hamstring trouble. He was compared to Neil Franklin - as a constructive central-defender who liked to play the ball out of defence. City supporters were able to enjoy that style of play coupled with a touch of steel that is necessary in all successful players during McFarland's brief spell at Valley Parade, which saw him make 47 League and Cup appearances for the club. In all, McFarland made 577 senior appearances, including 434 League matches for Derby.

McFarland, rated by many people as the classiest England defender in the post-war era, arrived at Valley Parade when City's fortunes were at a low ebb. After missing out on promotion on goal difference the season before, the club had endured what could politely be described as a flat season, which culminated in a drab 1-0 home defeat against Hereford United in May 1981 watched by City's lowest ever crowd – 1,249.

The crowd – if that is the correct way to describe such a small gathering – included McFarland as he was deciding whether to take up the offer of player-manager. Fortunately for City, he was not put off by that performance, recruited his former Derby teammate Mick Jones as assistant manager and together they transformed the team and led the club to promotion the following season.

City soon established themselves as one of the promotion favourites after a run of nine successive wins to equal a club record and eventually finish in second place, five points behind the division's outstanding team, Sheffield United.

They had made a decent start to the new season back in the Third Division when supporters were shocked to find that McFarland and Jones had handed in their resignations. They walked out on the club one November afternoon, 24 hours after City had beaten Port Vale away in a first-round FA Cup tie. Two days later they were installed as part of a new look management team at Derby as the club tried to recreate the great days under Brian Clough. Peter Taylor, Brian Clough's right-hand man in Derby's great days of a decade earlier, was appointed general manager with McFarland as team manager assisted by Jones.

The move turned out to be a failure, Peter Taylor left the club, leaving McFarland with nine games to save Derby from relegation. He couldn't do it, but he stayed on to help former chief scout Arthur Cox lead Derby back up. McFarland continued his managerial career at Bolton where he was joint manager with former Derby teammate and future City manager Colin Todd and later managed Cambridge United and Torquay United before becoming manager at Chesterfield in 2003, but in March 2007, with relegation looming, he was sacked.

Andy McGill

Date of birth: 11 July 1924
Died: 1988

Bradford City record:
Appearances: League 164, FA Cup 9
Goals: League 24, FA Cup 3
Debut: 8 November 1947 v Darlington

Also played for: Florida Arms, Third Lanark, Queen's Park, Clyde, Scunthorpe United

Scot Andy McGill was a driving force for Bradford City for five seasons in the immediate post World War Two period. McGill would drive on his teammates from his favoured right-half – midfield – position in modern football. A natural leader and organiser on the field, it was natural that he should become captain and teammates would feel the wrath of his tongue if they didn't show the commitment that he, himself, was prepared to offer to the side.

McGill was born in Glasgow and played with junior club Florida Amateurs before moving into League football with Third Lanark and nearby Queen's Park Rangers. He joined Clyde after the war, before signing for City in November 1947 for £3,250, a month after his Clyde teammate, centre-forward John Neilson.

McGill immediately commanded a regular place in the side and played 164 League games in the Third Division North and nine FA Cup matches in his five seasons at Valley Parade, scoring 27 League Cup goals.

It wasn't a particularly successful period in the club's history as City tried to rebuild after the war, and in 1948–49 they suffered the indignity of having to seek re-election for the first time in their history.

McGill left City in July 1952 to join their Third Division North rivals Scunthorpe United in a £2,500 deal and played a similar role as he captained a young side, making 183 League appearances and scoring 15 goals in five years at the club's old venue – the Old Show Ground – before retiring in 1957.

Ironically, Scunthorpe gained promotion to the Second Division the year after McGill retired. He settled in Lincolnshire and worked as a sales representative in the wines and spirits trade. He died in 1988, aged 64.

Jim McLaren

Date of birth: 1897
Died: 1975

Bradford City record:
Appearances: League 155, FA Cup 6
Debut: 5 May 1923 v Clapton Orient

Also played for: Stenhousemuir, Leicester City, Watford

Scot Jim McLaren is undoubtedly one of the best goalkeepers to have played for Bradford City, and his agility, positional sense and strong physical presence served him well in a 20-year League career in Scotland and England. Born in Falkirk in 1897, the son of a Scottish champion racing cyclist, McLaren thought of following in his father's footsteps but turned to football, and in 1911 he played in Scotland's first Schoolboy international and distinguished himself with a penalty save against England.

World War One interrupted his football plans as he served with the Argyll and Sutherland Highlanders in France, but he managed to play for the regiment and when the war was over he joined Stenhousemuir, helping them into the Scottish League and through their first season before joining City.

McLaren joined City from Stenhousemuir in May 1922, just as they were relegated from the First Division. He made only one appearance in the following season but gained a regular place in the side after that, when fellow Scot Jock Ewart left to rejoin Airdrieonians, playing in all 42 League matches in the 1923-24 campaign. In fact, such was McLaren's consistency that he missed only 12 League matches in four seasons before he left to join First Division Leicester City in May 1927, after making 161 League and FA Cup appearances for the club.

McLaren's five-year spell at Valley Parade covered a difficult period in the club's history as City struggled to regain their First Division status. They didn't, of course, and McLaren was reluctantly sold one week before the end of the 1926-27 season, with City facing relegation to the Third Division North. No doubt he was happy to miss the last match for it ended in a humiliating 8-0 defeat at Manchester City.

City did not want to sell such an accomplished goalkeeper, but they were facing one of their financial crises, and, sadly, not for the first time in their long history, they needed to sell one of their best players.

The move to Leicester proved to be good for McLaren as he displaced fellow Scot Kenny Campbell and helped his new club to make a serious assault on the First Division Championship. They didn't win the title, but were runners-up in his second season.

McLaren made 180 League and FA Cup appearances in his six and a half years at Leicester, until he was replaced by his fellow Scot and namesake Sandy McLaren. He then moved into the Third Division South with Watford in October 1933 and continued his consistent form, making more than 200 League and FA Cup appearances for them as they remained in the top six throughout his six-year stay. By the time he retired at the outbreak of World War Two he had played in 519 League matches.

By that time McLaren had turned 41, and he became only the second player in League history to receive five-year benefit payments from three clubs – Bradford City, Leicester City and Watford.

After retiring from football, he settled in Leicester and died there in 1975 aged 78.

David McNiven

Date of birth: 5 September 1955

Bradford City record:
Appearances: League 212, FA Cup 11, League Cup 22
Goals: League 64, FA Cup 2
Debut: 25 February 1978 v Rotherham United

Also played for: Leeds United, Blackpool, Pittsburgh, Halifax Town, Morecambe

Striker David McNiven has a special place in Bradford City's history, becoming the club's record signing when he joined them in February 1978 for £25,000 from Leeds United. In fact, the transfer record was broken twice that day. Full-back Mick Wood set a new record when he joined them from Blackburn Rovers for £15,000, but the record was broken less than three hours later when McNiven signed.

It was one of those rare periods in their history when the club had money to spend in the transfer market thanks to the success of their weekly lottery – at one stage they were selling 60,000 tickets a week – and McNiven looked to be an exciting prospect. Perhaps he didn't fulfil all his expectations, but McNiven still enjoyed an average of one goal in every three League matches, and by the time he left Valley Parade five years later he had scored 64 League goals in 212 matches.

Born at Stonehouse near Glasgow, he played for Scotland Schoolboys before he became an apprentice at Leeds then signed professional forms in 1972 when the team that Don Revie created was still one of the top three sides in England. In the face of fierce competition from established internationals, it was not surprising that McNiven had to wait until 1976 for his League debut, scoring a goal against Manchester City after coming on as a substitute. McNiven gained Under-21 caps for Scotland, but despite being a prolific goalscorer for United's reserve and junior sides, he failed to gain a regular first-team place at Elland Road and joined City.

The side were in big trouble when McNiven arrived, having lost seven matches in a row, and were in grave danger of relegation after winning promotion the season before. He made an immediate impact, his pace proving to be too much for Third Division defences, and scored in his opening match at Plymouth, but the match was abandoned because of a blizzard 25 minutes from the end, with City leading 1–0. McNiven scored the following Saturday, helping City to beat Rotherham at home 3–0, and managed five goals in 18 matches to the end of the season, but it was not enough to save them from relegation.

McNiven was leading scorer for the next two seasons – 15 goals in 1978–79 and 17 goals in 1979–80 when City finished in fifth place, missing out on promotion on goal average under George Mulhall. His tally dipped to eight goals in 1980–81, but he enjoyed an outstanding season in 1981–82 when City gained promotion from the Fourth Division under player-manager Roy McFarland. A small, somewhat stocky but quick striker, McNiven was the perfect foil for the strong and competitive Bobby Campbell, and their partnership was a crucial element in City gaining promotion in second place behind champions Sheffield United. They scored 43 League goals, with Campbell netting 24 and McNiven 19, including all four goals in City's 4–1 win over Crewe three matches before the end of the season.

McNiven didn't do as well the following campaign, and three months after he arrived as player-manager his former Leeds United teammate Trevor Cherry allowed him to leave and he joined Blackpool on a free transfer in February 1983. He then had a spell in the United States in the NASL with Pittsburgh Spirit before returning to England to join Halifax Town in March 1985. At the end of that season he moved to Morecambe and finished his career there.

Looking back on his Valley Parade career, McNiven said 'I thought George Mulhall was very unlucky. He was a good manager, but he didn't get the resources he needed to build the team. We let him down on the last day of the 1979–80 season when we lost at Peterborough – we only needed a point to win promotion and after that there was no back for us.

'Roy McFarland and his assistant Mick Jones were like a breath of fresh air when they came in. I was unsettled at that time. I was in a rut and I felt I had to get away to try to do something, but Roy created an exceptional season and that was the highlight of my career at Bradford. The partnership I had with Bobby Campbell was fantastic.

'When Roy left and Trevor Cherry came in I felt I needed a change and things were not very good. It was probably my fault – I should have given Trevor a chance. He wanted to change my position, but I didn't want to do it. I should have tried to fit in with his plans, but, there again, I wouldn't have had a move to Blackpool and we have been happy here for more than 20 years.'

McNiven, who lives at St Annes, works at Preston, running the commercial department at Evans Halshaw, the Ford arm of Pendragon – the largest motor distributor in Europe. He plays golf and squash and watches as much football as he can – his twin sons, David and Scott, who were born not long after he moved to Bradford, both play professional football.

John Middleton

Date of birth: 11 July 1955

Bradford City record:
Appearances: League 192, FA Cup 11, League Cup 11
Goals: League 5, FA Cup 1
Debut: 23 April 1973 v Doncaster Rovers

Also played for: Macclesfield Town

He wasn't particularly tall for a central-defender in the lower divisions – nor was his partner David Fretwell – but John Middleton was an effective and consistent player for Bradford City for five seasons in the 1970s. Born at Rawmarsh in South Yorkshire, Middleton joined City as a 16-year-old amateur in December 1971 after being recommended by his elder brother Peter, who was established as a first-team player at Valley Parade at that time.

After becoming an apprentice professional in January 1972, Middleton signed as a full-time professional in July 1973, the day after his 18th birthday. By that time he had made two League appearances, making his debut in a 4-3 home win over Doncaster Rovers before playing in the last match of the season at home to Southport five days later. However, he made only three League appearances the following season, and it was not until the season after that – 1974-75 – that he was able to command a regular place in the side. He played in 40 League matches that season, starting his partnership with Fretwell, and he was a regular for the next five seasons until his Valley Parade career wound down in 1979.

Middleton missed only four matches in 1975-76 and played in all six FA Cup matches that season, including the giant killing 2-1 win at Norwich City and the 1-0 defeat against eventual winners Southampton – the first time City had reached the quarter-final for 56 years. He was also at the forefront of the club's successful Fourth Division promotion campaign in 1976-77, missing only five matches as they went up in fourth place and played in 40 matches the season after that as City came straight back down again.

Middleton's fortunes changed during the following season as George Mulhall replaced John Napier as manager in the November. He began the new season with Steve Baines as his new defensive partner, Fretwell having moved to Wigan Athletic, while Baines had joined the club two months before the end of the previous campaign in a £17,000 deal from Huddersfield Town. However, Middleton was no longer a regular player in the second half of the season as Mulhall rang the changes. Mick Wood was switched from left-back to partner Baines at the centre of the defence for some matches, Terry Dolan also moved from midfield to play in a defensive role on occasions, and future skipper, 18-year-old defender Peter Jackson, was given his debut in the last two months of the season.

Middleton left City at the end of the season to join non-League Macclesfield Town, having made 214 League and Cup appearances for the club, including 192 in the League. He never played League football again, despite the fact that he was only 24 when he left Valley Parade and later became a licensee at Otley.

His brother Peter left City in September 1972 to join Plymouth Argyle in a exchange deal that brought midfield player Ronnie Brown to Valley Parade, and he scored on his debut, but that proved to be his only appearance for Plymouth because a few days later he was struck by a car and suffered injuries that were to end his career. He played in the reserves in an attempt to make a comeback before he was forced to retire on medical advice, and he died in tragic circumstances in April 1977, aged a mere 28.

Brian Mitchell

Date of birth: 16 July 1963

Bradford City record:
Appearances: League 178, FA Cup 7, League Cup 21
Goals: League 9, FA Cup 1
Debut: 14 February 1987 v Crystal Palace

Also played for: Aberdeen, Bristol City, Hull City

If Bradford City supporters don't remember Brian Mitchell's five-year spell at Valley Parade for anything else they will never forget his winning goal against Tottenham Hotspur in the FA Cup third round in January 1989, and nor will he. It was the highlight of his career at Valley Parade and the former Scottish Schoolboy international remembers it vividly.

Mick Kennedy played the ball short to Mitchell on the right-hand side of the penalty area, and he scored with a low shot into the far corner. 'I struck it well into the corner of the net past Bobby Mimms in the Spurs goal', he recalls. 'I wasn't sure whether the referee would blow for taking the kick too early. Unfortunately, Sutton beat Chelsea so we were not the main match on Match of the Day, but it was one of those games that I will never forget and I will never reach that pinnacle again.'

Unfortunately for City, they lost 2-1 at home to Hull City in a far less demanding fourth-round tie three weeks later, and two days after that manager Terry Dolan and his assistant Stan Ternent lost their jobs.

It was Dolan who tempted Mitchell to try his luck in English football when he joined City from Aberdeen for a then club record £70,000 fee in February 1987, and he immediately established himself in the team. He played every match to the end of that season, after making his debut in a 1-1 draw at Crystal Palace, and missed only two matches the following campaign as City missed out on promotion after being beaten in the Play-offs.

'It was a big move for me because Aberdeen were flying high, but Alex Ferguson had gone to Manchester United and I didn't see eye to eye with the new manager Ian Porterfield. I heard Bradford City were interested in me and I spoke to Terry Dolan.

'The English League was a fantastic stage on which to play football and signing for Bradford was the best move I ever made. I was a full-back who liked to get forward so the way City played suited my style of game, and I adapted really well and I enjoyed it. There is more of a challenge in English football. In the Scottish League you play the same team four times a season and apart from the big games against Rangers and Celtic it can be hard to raise your game. The speed of the game in Scotland is slower than in England and there is more quality in England.

'When I came to Bradford I found myself facing fantastic clubs with historic traditions with high-profile names. We had a great bunch of lads at Valley Parade – all of a similar age – and I had a good three years there, but I had a few problems after that and I became a bit unsettled. I had knee problems which affected me, and I had five knee operations on my cartilage. Obviously, the highlights for me were the Spurs Cup win and getting to the League Cup quarter-finals by beating Everton at Valley Parade. Then there was the disappointment of losing the last game of the 1987-88 season against Ipswich, and then being beaten by Middlesbrough in the Play-offs – that will never leave me.'

So, after making 178 League appearances for City over a five-year spell, Mitchell left Valley Parade in July 1992 to join Bristol City. 'I had just over a year at Ashton Gate', he said. 'It was a new challenge and there were some good players, including a young Andy Cole, Leroy Rosenior – later manager at Torquay and Brentford – and Russell Osman. We had a strong team in the old Second Division, but I didn't really adapt to the south west of England, and I went to Hull to join Terry Dolan. Unfortunately, I only spent six months there because my knee injury troubled me again – it was a disappointing end to my career.'

Mitchell played 14 games in Europe for Aberdeen, including a European Cup quarter-final, but added 'Although I played 165 games for them, for most of the time I was in and out of the side.'

Mitchell is now back in Aberdeen, working as a manager organising sport and physical activities in 20 schools in partnership with Sport Scotland and Aberdeenshire County Council and also works in partnership with Aberdeen FC – they deliver the coaching in conjunction with the county council. 'I am close to the club and a member of their strong ex-players' association. I was a football development manager when I retired from football. I also went coaching in the US and then got a degree at Glasgow Caledonian University in leisure management, and I later got a post graduate degree at Aberdeen University. I went back to the US, but I thought I wasn't using my academic qualifications so I returned to take my present job.'

Charlie Moore

Date of birth: 1905
Died: December 1972

Bradford City record:
Appearances: League 339, FA Cup 29
Goals: League 53, FA Cup 7
Debut: 18 December 1926 v Manchester City

Also played for: Manton Colliery

Nottinghamshire-born Charlie Moore was a player of genuine stature at Valley Parade for 14 seasons up to the outbreak of World War Two, playing in a variety of positions. He was a loyal club man and popular with his teammates, and by the time he retired in 1940, aged 35, he had made 339 League appearances – at that time, second only to George Robinson, whose consistency in City's first 12 seasons set the standard for others to follow.

Born in Worksop, Moore joined City from Manton Colliery in 1926 in what turned out to be a depressing season as the club finished bottom of the Second Division, five years after losing their First Division status, and made his mark as an inside-forward.

He had the pleasure of playing alongside his brother Fred, who returned to non-League football with Worksop after just four months at the club. For brother Charlie, however, that first season was the start of a long and fruitful relationship with what turned out to be his only League club, and he settled in the Bradford area when his career was over, dying at Shipley in December 1972 aged 67.

Moore scored eight goals in 18 League matches in his first season and did even better the following campaign when he switched to centre-forward, as City played their first Third Division campaign. He was top scorer with 16 goals in 32 League matches as City finished sixth, but he managed only 14 games the following season as he was replaced in the second half by Bert Whitehurst, who joined them from Liverpool in February 1929. Whitehorse exploded on to the Valley Parade scene with an extraordinary tally of 24 goals in the last 15 matches of the season as City won the Third Division North Championship by scoring 128 goals – a record for a 42-match programme. Moore also managed seven goals in 14 League matches and four in the FA Cup, including a hat-trick in a first-round home win over Doncaster Rovers.

Moore eventually settled into a dependable half-back, although he sometimes played on the left wing as he became a regular during City's Second Division campaigns in the 1930s and then when they dropped back into the Third Division in 1937. In the last two seasons before the war, he missed only five matches in 1937–38 and three in 1938–39, but the hostilities cut short his career. He scored 11 goals in 28 League matches in 1931–32, but the goals dried up after that as he played more games at half-back, but he still ended his career with 53 League goals and seven in the Cup, taking his tally to 60 League and Cup goals in 368 League and Cup appearances – a fine record.

George Mulholland

Date of birth: 4 August 1928
Died: January 2002

Bradford City record:
Appearances: League 277, FA Cup 27
Debut: 29 August 1953 v Chesterfield

Also played for: Stoke City, Darlington

Bradford City have had few more popular or consistent players than George Mulholland. In fact, such was his level of consistency that he made 246 consecutive appearances between August 1953 and September 1958, beating the record held by an equally consistent player, right-back Charlie Bicknell. Not surprisingly, he has an honoured place in the club's hall of fame set up in the museum at Valley Parade.

Mulholland, who was born in Ayr, moved to the Potteries with his family when he was only two. He served in the Royal Navy during World War Two, but it was not until 1949–50 season that he joined Stoke City as an amateur. He became a full-time professional in July 1950, but failed to become a first-team regular and made only three League appearances in three years before player-manager Ivor Powell signed him for City on a free transfer in July 1953. It was a superb piece of business. His remarkable run for City started on 29 August 1953 and only ended on 1 September 1958 when he suffered a fractured leg 12 minutes from the end of a match at Mansfield.

Mulholland had two regular full-back partners, first Scotsman Jock Whyte and then Tom Flockett, when he joined City from Chesterfield in 1956, and for most of his matches goalkeeper Geoff Smith played behind him.

Geoff Smith played in 200 consecutive league matches between 1954 and 1958, and like Mulholland he was an ever present in four consecutive seasons. He said 'George was a good friend. He deserved to play in a better standard of football because he was so fast. No one could get past him. They used to turn George and thought they had beaten him, but he could catch pigeons. He was really too good for that division. I am surprised he never made it at a higher level. He was an honest professional. He did his job and enjoyed it.'

It was Mulholland's extraordinary powers of recovery that most City supporters will remember. The term wing-back had not been thought of when Mulholland plied his trade at Valley Parade. He was a full-back whose function was to defend and specifically to mark and stop his opposing winger. The notion of a full-back running down the flank and delivering a cross into the goalmouth was to come later. However, although he was not a wing-back, Mulholland had the principal quality modern players who operate in that position need most – pace – and he used his pace to considerable effect as a defender. Sometimes his opponent would go past him, but more often than not Mulholland would recover to make the vital tackle or manage to play the ball safely into touch.

He made 304 League and FA Cup appearances for City – 277 in the League and 27 in the Cup – before he left for Darlington on a free transfer in July 1960, and he made more than 100 League appearances for them before retiring in July 1963. When his career ended three years later, he settled at Billingham on Teesside, but he never forgot his seven-year spell at Valley Parade.

His son David, who was born while his father played for City, said 'My father had fond memories of his years at Bradford City. He had a couple of scrapbooks from his City days and always looked for their results. He loved his time at Bradford. Dad liked to be busy, and when his football career was over he worked in various jobs. He worked at the ICI at Billingham, and he was also a school caretaker and insurance agent.'

Mulholland died in January 2002 aged 73 after a four-year battle against cancer.

George Murphy

Date of birth: 22 July 1915
Died: December 1983

Bradford City record:
Appearances: League 180, FA Cup 10
Goals: League 43, FA Cup 3
Debut: 8 December 1934 v Bury

Also played for: Hull City, Scunthorpe United

One of the most popular players either side of World War Two was ginger-haired Welshman George Murphy, whose nickname was inevitably 'Spud'. A strong, whole hearted player, he appeared in virtually every position for the club – inside-forward, half-back, full-back or centre-forward, but mainly at full-back or centre-forward – and played under five managers in his 13 years at Valley Parade.

A great servant for City, Murphy made 190 League and FA Cup appearances spread over eight seasons in peacetime, scoring 46 goals. He also made most wartime appearances for the club, playing in 128 matches and scoring 42 goals, two more appearances than future Newcastle player and manager Joe Harvey, who also scored 39 goals. It is said that Murphy played for eight different clubs in a nine-week period during wartime.

Spud also played for Wales in two unofficial internationals in the 1943–44 season, and it was a shame that, like so many of his generation, he reached his peak during the war, in which he served in the RAF. The war spanned seven seasons and that is a huge part of any footballer's career.

He joined City as a 19-year-old in 1934 after playing for two junior sides in Newport, Ponthlenfoith and Cwmfelinfach and made his debut in a Second Division home match against Bury in December that year. For most of his first two seasons, Murphy played at inside-left and continued in that position in 1936–37, but switched to centre-forward in the closing weeks of the campaign as City battled unsuccessfully against relegation and scored four goals in the last eight matches.

Murphy's best season was in 1938–39 – the last full season before the war – making 41 appearances mainly at right-back as City made a realistic bid for promotion from the Third Division North, finishing in third place.

Spud returned to centre-forward after the war, scoring 14 goals in 30 matches in 1946–47, and he made a great start to the following season, scoring four goals in the first three matches, but after scoring seven goals in 16 matches he was surprisingly transferred to Hull City in December 1947 in a £1,500 deal.

He scored nine goals in 15 appearances for the Tigers in the second half of the 1947–48 season before he was transferred to Scunthorpe United – then in the Midland League – the following August. He played more non-League football with Scarborough and Goole Town before ending his career.

Murphy became a publican in Humberside when his career was over but later returned to West Yorkshire as a club steward at Morley and died at his home at nearby Tingley in December 1983, aged 68, after being dogged by ill health.

Graham Oates

Date of birth: 14 March 1949

Bradford City record:
Appearances: League 161, FA Cup 10, League Cup 4
Goals: League 19, FA Cup 2
Debut: 4 April 1970 v Walsall

Also played for: Manningham Mills, Blackburn Rovers, Newcastle United, Detroit Express, Gainsborough Trinity

Graham Oates came to Bradford City through local football and went on to play at the top level with Newcastle United. Bradford-born Oates showed good ball control for a tall player but was very much in the gentle giant mould, and one wonders how things would have turned out for him if he had been able to show more aggression in his play.

Oates played his early football with local Bradford sides Tong Street and Manningham Mills before leaving his job as a cloth manufacturer to join Bradford City, signing first as an amateur in November 1969 when he was 20 before becoming a full-time professional three months later. He made his debut in the Third Division as centre-half in a 2–0 defeat at Walsall in April 1970 and also played in the 3–3 home draw against Barrow the following week.

Oates played five matches at centre-half early the following season, deputising for Tom Hallett, but reappeared the following season at centre-forward in an attempt to solve City's goalscoring problems, and he scored six goals in 20 consecutive appearances to the end of the season.

He gained a regular place at centre-half the following season following Hallett's retirement, missing only two matches, and although City again used him at centre-forward in the closing stages of the campaign, as they became desperate for goals to try to avoid relegation – they managed only five in the last nine matches, four of them in one match, a 4–1 win at Plymouth – and they finished in last place.

Oates again played at centre-half in the early matches of the following season, but following the signing of Northern Ireland international John Napier from Brighton, he developed into a midfield player, missing only three matches. City were looking to bounce straight back into the Third Division but finished a disappointing 16th, although they did enjoy a run in the FA Cup, beating Second Division Blackpool 2–1 at home before being knocked out by Arsenal in a 2–0 defeat at Highbury.

Oates missed only two matches the following season, scoring eight goals, as City did better, finishing eighth without ever threatening promotion, but again they reached the FA Cup fourth round before losing 3–0 at Luton. This turned out to be Oates's last season at Valley Parade as manager Bryan Edwards arranged a player-exchange deal in the 1974 close season,

with Oates moving to Third Division Blackburn Rovers and winger Don Hutchins coming to Valley Parade plus £15,000 in cash for City.

Oates played in 175 League and Cup matches, scoring 21 goals in his five seasons at Valley Parade, and missed only one match as Blackburn won the Third Division Championship in his first season at Ewood Park. He was also an ever present in Blackburn's Second Division team the following season, until Newcastle signed him along with goalkeeper Roger Jones in March 1976.

Oates scored 10 goals in 76 League matches in nearly two seasons at Blackburn, but he was not nearly as successful at Newcastle and left during the 1977–78 season, after making 35 League appearances, nine of them as a substitute. He turned down a loan move to Sheffield Wednesday and headed for the US to join the NASL club Detroit Express for £40,000 in March 1978. He returned to City in 1981 as a non-contract player but went back to America after only two reserve matches. He later played in Bradford for Lidget Green and played and managed Dudley Hill Athletic, and he also turned out for Gainsborough Trinity.

Andrew O'Brien

Date of birth: 29 June 1979

Bradford City record:
Appearances: League 133, FA Cup 8, League Cup 5
Goals: League 3, FA Cup 1
Debut: 16 October 1996 v Queen's Park Rangers

Also played for: Newcastle United, Portsmouth, Bolton Wanderers

One of Bradford City's best young players of the modern era is Andrew O'Brien, who has already played Premiership football for three clubs – including the Bantams. The central-defender made his debut as a 17-year-old in October 1996 – six months after City had gained promotion through the Play-offs at Wembley – and he helped them to gain promotion to the Premiership before playing more top flight football with Newcastle United and Portsmouth.

O'Brien, who was born at Harrogate, was on York City's books as a youngster and then had a trial at Leeds United before joining City as a 15-year-old.

Brian Peet, who helped to look after City's schoolboys in those days, signed O'Brien, and he then came under the wing of youth-team manager Steve Smith before manager Chris Kamara handed him his first-team debut at Queen's Park Rangers. 'I remember Trevor Sinclair scored the winner for QPR in the last minute,' he recalled.

O'Brien went on to gain a regular place in the side and helped them to win promotion to the Premiership in 1998-99, but the game which stands out in his memory is the last match of the first Premiership season in May 2000.

'I have been privileged to play in some memorable games, but I think the Bradford-Liverpool match was the most memorable,' he said. 'I have been privileged to be challenging at the top of the League, but also at the bottom. I remember we beat our rivals Wimbledon at home two weeks before the end of the season, and then we lost at Leicester, which meant we had our Premiership future to play for while Liverpool had a Champions League place to play for.

'Southampton played Wimbledon on the same day, and we knew if we beat Liverpool it would give us the best opportunity of survival. Ultimately, David Wetherall's header from a corner in the 12th minute gave us a 1-0 win and we survived, whereas Liverpool finished fifth, just outside the top four Champions League places.

'I look back on my time at Bradford with a lot of good memories. I joined the club as an apprentice and we got promoted through Play-offs at Wembley; Chris Kamara gave me my debut the following season when we just managed to stay up, and two years later we won promotion to the Premiership under Paul Jewell and then stayed up on the last day of the season.

'I will always be very grateful to Wayne Jacobs, who helped me through an unsettling period when I left school to scrape his boots. Stuart McCall was also a big influence when he returned to the club, as was David Wetherall when he joined us from Leeds United. There were a lot of good people there. Jamie Lawrence had a chequered past, but he worked hard to get us back on track on the football field – he would run through a brick wall for you.'

O'Brien was on the move near transfer deadline day in City's second season in the Premiership, joining Newcastle in a £1.5 million deal as the Bantams were clearly destined for relegation. 'I was fortunate to get a move to Newcastle,' said O'Brien. 'I remember we were preparing to play Manchester City when I was called into chairman Geoffrey Richmond's office, and he told me the club had accepted a £1.5 million offer from Newcastle, and he asked me if I wanted to speak to them. That put me out of the Manchester City game and I watched the game from the stand and then drove to Newcastle the following day and signed for them.

Graeme Souness succeeded Robson when the former England manager was sacked just four matches into the 2004-05 season, and at the end of that season O'Brien moved to Portsmouth despite having three years left on a four-year contract at St James' Park. The club had young players coming through, of whom Newcastle had high expectations, and Souness had indicated that he would not be automatic first choice.

O'Brien said 'I was impressed with manager Alan Perrin when I went to Portsmouth, but he only lasted 12 games and Harry Redknapp took over. I played 33 League games in the 2005-06 season and played in some big matches like Fulham, West Ham and Manchester City as we managed to stay up, but I missed the last seven games with a back injury.'

O'Brien is also enjoying a successful career with the Republic of Ireland, for whom he qualifies through his grandparents, his father's parents, who were born in County Limerick, but lost his place at Portsmouth in 2006-07. He has since signed a two-year contract for Bolton Wanderers.

Gavin Oliver

Date of birth: 6 September 1962

Bradford City record:
Appearances: League 313, FA Cup 16, League Cup 30
Goals: League 9, League Cup 2
Debut: 23 November 1985 v Shrewsbury Town

Also played for: Sheffield Wednesday, Tranmere Rovers (loan), Brighton & Hove Albion (loan)

No club could wish for a more conscientious player than Gavin Oliver, who was a consistent defender for a decade before injury hastened his retirement in 1995. Oliver arrived at Valley Parade from Sheffield Wednesday in November 1985 as newly-promoted City were trying to establish themselves in the Second Division after winning the Third Division Championship six months earlier.

It was a difficult time for the club as Bradford mourned the loss of 56 lives in the fire tragedy as well as trying to cope with higher division football without a home of their own – City played at Odsal Stadium, Huddersfield Town and Leeds United while decisions were being made in the redevelopment of fire-wrecked Valley Parade.

Oliver began his Valley Parade career at right-back, and it soon became clear that the £20,000 City paid to Wednesday was money well spent. He immediately established himself as a regular and invaluable member of the side, first at right-back and later in the centre of the defence. He played the remaining 27 matches at right-back in his first season before he eventually replaced Peter Jackson in the centre of the defence after the City captain moved to Newcastle United in October 1986.

Oliver, who was born at Felling in the North East, began his career as a schoolboy centre-forward before joining Sheffield Wednesday to work on the ground in 1979. An injury to the centre-half in a junior match saw him switched to the defence, and that is where he spent the rest of his career. He signed full-time professional forms for Wednesday in 1980 and made his League debut one month later as a substitute at Oldham, but he did not make his full League debut until three years later when he went on loan to Fourth Division Tranmere Rovers in January 1983.

Oliver returned to Hillsborough in April 1983, but he still found his first-team chances limited, and in August 1985 he went to Brighton for another loan spell. The move to the south coast turned out to be a good one for Oliver because he played in Brighton's first 16 matches of the season before joining City.

City were able to give Oliver something he had not enjoyed in his five years at Wednesday – regular first-team football – and in the next three seasons he missed only five matches, forming a good understanding with Dave Evans when Jackson moved to Newcastle and then with Lee Sinnott when Evans became sweeper.

Oliver said 'I had been on loan at Brighton when I joined Bradford. I remember it was a difficult time for the club after the fire tragedy. We were playing at Odsal, Huddersfield and Leeds, which wasn't ideal from any point of view, but it wasn't just disruptive for the players and supporters. The Valley Parade disaster was a massive tragedy and there were other issues in the background.

'It was a difficult time for everyone, including Trevor Cherry and Terry Yorath, who were having to put a team together while playing at three different grounds, but from the time I joined the club there was a camaraderie from all quarters, players and supporters who had seen so much from the disaster. Everyone pulled together and looked after each other and got others through it – it was a happy, family club. I didn't witness what happened at the fire, but it was very emotional even from watching it on television and the subsequent publicity. Everyone was touched by what had happened.

'I started at right-back, which wasn't my favourite position, but eventually I nailed down a place at centre-half. It was a happy time. Over a 10-year period you have your ups and downs, but you look at players who stayed for a long period like Mark Ellis, Greg Abbott, Paul Tomlinson and myself – it was that sort of club.

'Unfortunately, after we failed to gain promotion in 1988 John Hendrie and Stuart McCall left and the team fell apart. If we had got promotion that season and money had been provided for strengthening it would have been interesting to see how that team could have progressed in the top division.'

Ian Ormondroyd

Date of birth: 22 September 1964

Bradford City record:
Appearances: League 125, FA Cup 10, League Cup 21
Goals: League 26, FA Cup 3, League Cup 7
Debut: 23 November 1985 v Shrewsbury Town

Also played for: Oldham Athletic (loan), Aston Villa, Derby County, Leicester City, Hull City (loan), Oldham Athletic, Scunthorpe United

The first thing you notice about Ian Ormondroyd is his height. At 6ft 4in tall he seems to tower over everyone – Liverpool striker Peter Crouch has a similar appearance and presence – and you assume he will be ungainly. However, Ormondroyd, known affectionately as Sticks, was exceptionally skilful on the ground and played many of his best matches on the wing rather than in a traditional centre-forward role, which you would assume to be his natural position.

Nowadays most players come into the professional game by way of youth schemes that can begin when prospective players are mere children, but Ormondroyd was spotted by City playing local football as a 20-year-old.

He went on to enjoy a 13-year career, which started with City in 1985, and he played at the top level with big clubs – Aston Villa, Derby County and Leicester. He played in four Play-off Finals, two as a winner, two as a loser, including three in successive seasons with Leicester.

Ormondroyd, who is now Football in the Community Officer at Bradford City, said 'It is rare for a player like me to come into professional football a couple of weeks before I was 21 – in September 1985 – after playing local league football for Manningham Mills and Thackley.

'It was a strange season because we played at three different grounds the season after the Valley Parade fire – Odsal, Huddersfield Town and Leeds United. I made my debut as substitute in a 2-0 defeat at Shrewsbury in November 1985 and scored my first goal in a 3-0 win against Huddersfield Town at Odsal the following March.

'I believe the game that really made me, however, was an FA Cup third-round replay against Oldham at Valley Parade in January 1987, just over a week after Trevor Cherry had been sacked. Terry Dolan had taken over as caretaker manager and had guided the team to a 1-1 draw in the Cup at Oldham.'

The replay was played on an icy pitch and City adapted themselves far better to the conditions as they raced into a 5-0 half-time lead with Ormondroyd enjoying a memorable game as he scored twice. He remembers one of the goals as being one of the best in his career. 'I took the ball down the right wing before cutting in along the by-line and slipping it under goalkeeper Andy Goram,' he said.

Oldham manager Joe Royle was impressed and, with City struggling to survive in Division Two, Dolan, by then confirmed as manager, decided to make changes on transfer deadline day. Among them was the loan transfer to the end of the season of Ormondroyd to Oldham while the experienced Ron Futcher came from Oldham to Valley Parade. 'It never really happened for me at Oldham where they had a plastic pitch,' said Ormondroyd, 'but we got to the Play-offs where we played Leeds United and were beaten over two legs.'

So, after losing in the Play-offs, City faced another season of Second Division football, but Ormondroyd got the big breakthrough to the top division the following February when he joined Aston Villa, managed by future England boss Graham Taylor, in a £650,000 deal. The deal happened in an eventful week at Valley Parade that began with City sacking Dolan and persuading Terry Yorath to join the club from Swansea.

Ormondroyd said 'I needed to do it – it was the best thing I could have done. We struggled at first, but the following season we brought in a few players and finished second, although we could have won the League. We were seven points clear with eight games to go, but we lost to Wimbledon at home and won only one of our last seven games. Liverpool came with a run and won the Championship by about 10 points.

'We got into the UEFA Cup and did well before we lost over two legs to Inter Milan. It was a great experience playing there. I left to go to Derby County for six months. I had a really good time there with Arthur Cox as manager and I felt I did really well with nine goals in 20 matches, but Lionel Pickering came in as chairman and I had to go because they wanted to sign Paul Kitson from Leicester.

'So, I went to Leicester which was a decent move and I played in three Play-off Finals in successive seasons. The first two we lost, but then we beat Derby to get into the Premiership. Then our manager Brian Little went to Villa and Mark McGhee came to Leicester. He didn't see me as the player he wanted and I went on loan to Hull with my old Bradford manager Terry Dolan. Then I came back to Leicester for a short time before I returned to Valley Parade with Gavin Ward and Nicky Mohan.

In his first season back at City he helped the club to win promotion through the Play-offs, coming on as a substitute in the Final at Wembley.

Frank O'Rourke

Date of birth: 1878
Died: 24 December 1954

Bradford City record:
Appearances: League 192, FA Cup 20
Goals: League 88, FA Cup 5
Debut: 6 April 1907 v Nottingham Forest

Also played for: Airdrieonians (twice), Albion Rovers

Bradford City have made few better signings than Frank O'Rourke, but he joined the club in unusual circumstances.

The robust, bustling, hard shooting Scottish centre-forward played for Airedrieonians in a friendly at Valley Parade in April 1907 and so impressed were the City officials that they roused him from his bed in a Leeds hotel that night to sign for the club.

O'Rourke, then 28, was an immediate success. He scored on his debut – a 2-1 defeat at Nottingham Forest – and scored both goals in a 2-0 home win against Lincoln City the following Saturday. In all he notched four goals in five matches to the end of the season, which gave City supporters a clear indication of what a good player the club had signed.

O'Rourke was then at his peak and he was top scorer in three of the next four campaigns. In his first full season, he missed only two League matches when he was leading scorer with 21 goals in 36 games as City won promotion to the First Division as Second Division champions just five years after they were formed. His personal highlight was the four goals he scored in City's 7-1 thrashing of Gainsborough Trinity in October 1907.

Then, he played just as important a role in keeping the club in the top flight. The only player to appear in every match, O'Rourke was again top scorer with 19 goals in 38 League matches, including six in the last six matches, among them a priceless goal as City beat Manchester United 1-0 in a tense final game of the season in front of a packed 30,000-plus crowd at Valley Parade. City had to win to stay up, and O'Rourke's goal ensured that they did just that.

O'Rourke then played a key role as City established themselves in the top flight. He was second top scorer with 20 goals – Bob Whittingham scored 21 – in 1909-10 and his goals' tally included three hat-tricks – in the 3-1 home win at Bristol City, a 7-3 win at Middlesbrough on Christmas Day and a 3-3 draw at home to Newcastle United.

He was leading scorer again the following season with 13 goals in 32 matches, as City achieved their highest ever League placing – fifth in the top division – before winning the FA Cup. He played in all seven Cup matches and scored one of the goals as City beat Blackburn Rovers 3-0 in the semi-final at Bramall Lane.

O'Rourke's appearances began to tail off after that momentous season as his namesake, manager Peter O'Rourke, rang the changes. He scored four goals in 21 League matches in 1911-12 and one in four Cup matches as City were knocked by eventual winners Barnsley in the quarter-final after a second replay. He scored five goals in 18 League matches the following season and two in only seven the season after that. He didn't appear in a League match in 1914-15 – the last season before League football was suspended for four seasons because of the war – but played in an FA Cup replay at Norwich that season.

O'Rourke established an impressive record of 88 goals in 192 League matches – a record that stood for 69 years until it was broken by Bobby Campbell in 1984. He also scored five goals in 20 Cup matches. He had enjoyed a fine record in Scottish football before joining City, starting with Airdrieonians before joining Albion Rovers and then going back to Airdrieonians, where he won a Scottish Second Division Championship medal. He gained one Scottish cap just before he joined City and scored against Ireland.

After retiring from League football during World War One, O'Rourke continued to captain City's reserve side into his 40s, by then playing at centre-half until his playing contract was cancelled in 1922 – the year the club were relegated back to the Second Division. He was first-team trainer from 1922 until the end of the 1925-26 season when, at the age of 47, he returned to his birthplace, Bargeddie after 19 years' loyal and impressive service to the club. He died at Bargeddie on Christmas Eve 1954, aged 77.

Peter O'Rourke

Date of birth: 1876
Died: January 1956

Bradford City record:
Appearances: League 43, FA Cup 6
Goals: League 1
Debut: 5 September 1903 v Gainsborough Trinity

Also played for: Glasgow Celtic, Burnley, Lincoln City, Chesterfield
Managed: Bradford City (twice), Pontypridd, Dundee Hibernians, Bradford Park Avenue, Walsall, Llanelly

Peter O'Rourke was one of the first players to sign for the new Bradford City in 1903, but it is as the club's most successful manager that he will be remembered – and celebrated. O'Rourke did not play in the club's first match, but was the regular centre-half in their first season and was still a player and captain when he succeeded Robert Campbell as manager in November 1905. His last match was in the FA Cup at Darlington the following month, after which he handed the centre-half position to Gerald Kirk and the captaincy to George Robinson.

He built the side that won the Second Division Championship in 1907-08 – an extraordinary achievement considering the fact that the club were formed only five years earlier. Within a year, however, he had to make wholesale changes to ensure that City managed to stay in the top flight – which they did after a tense 1-0 victory over Manchester United at Valley Parade in the final match of the season.

Undoubtedly, his greatest triumph came in 1911, when City won the FA Cup, beating Newcastle United 1-0 in a replay at Old Trafford, while also finishing fifth in the First Division – their highest placing in the top flight. His managerial skills were shown to the full during the Cup Final. After City had earned a reply after a dour 0-0 draw at the Crystal Palace, O'Rourke made a crucial change for the replay at Old Trafford, bringing in Bob Torrance for Willie Gildea, who had not played well in the first match. At the same time, he made the brave decision to keep Peter Logan at outside-right even though England international Dickie Bond was free of suspension. The result justified the manager's decisions as City won 1-0 to bring the Cup back to Bradford.

O'Rourke continued to keep City around or just above halfway in the First Division up to World War One, but when football resumed after the hostilities it was clear that the club needed to rejuvenate the team. Changes were made, but they didn't have the desired result, and City were relegated in 1922. However, O'Rourke left the season before. Apparently the death of his son Francis in Newfoundland in October 1919 had a traumatic effect on him, and he resigned in June 1921.

He went to Wales to take charge of Pontypridd for five months and then became manager of Dundee Hibernians, but in April 1924 he returned to Bradford to become manager of Park Avenue. It was during his 10 months in charge at Park Avenue that another son, Peter – known to everyone as young Peter – made an explosive entry to League football, scoring twice in the first six minutes of his debut against Durham City. Sadly, illness cut short his football career.

O'Rourke later made a spectacular return to Valley Parade in May 1928 after the club had nearly gone out of business because of severe financial trouble. It was the year after City had been relegated to the Third Division North, but O'Rourke led them back to the Second Division as Third Division North champions with 128 goals – a record for a 42-match programme. He then left Valley Parade for a second time as City survived in their first season back in the Second Division, resigning in May 1930. He later managed Walsall and Llanelli before retiring in 1933. He died in January 1956, aged 82.

Senior players who played under him pay fulsome tribute to O'Rourke, who, apparently, was particularly skilled at man management. His greatest signing, England international winger Dickie Bond, paid this tribute, writing in the *Yorkshire Sports* nearly 40 years after O'Rourke signed him from Preston North End, 'I never think or talk much about my days with City without Peter O'Rourke coming into my mind. You can have your Chapmans or Allisons or Buckleys, but Peter was the greatest manager of them all. He knew just how to handle players, and he was an expert at selling them – those the club didn't really need and for good prices too.'

Harold Peel

Harold Peel

Date of birth: 1900
Died: January 1976

Bradford City record:
Appearances: League 186, FA Cup 13
Goals: League 26, FA Cup 1
Debut: 14 December 1929 v Blackpool

Also played for: Bradford Park Avenue, Arsenal

There is little doubt that Harold Peel was one of the best footballers the city of Bradford has ever produced. The skilful player, who operated on the left-hand side, either on the wing or at inside-forward, began his career with Park Avenue, who signed Peel as a professional in 1921 after spotting him playing for the Calverley junior club, and he made his League debut against Arsenal.

Coincidentally, Peel left Park Avenue for Arsenal five years later when he joined the Gunners for £1,750 in December 1926, after he had played a then record 226 League and Cup matches for Avenue, scoring 40 goals. After three years at Highbury, Peel, then 29, returned to Bradford, but this time to Valley Parade, joining City in a £1,100 deal in December 1929, six months after the Bantams won the Third Division North Championship under Peter O'Rourke.

Peel became an influential figure as City established themselves as a good class Second Division club. A natural leader, he became captain during his seven seasons at Valley Parade before retiring in 1936 after making 199 League and Cup appearances and scoring 27 goals. He scored 10 goals in 35 League matches in the 1931–32 season and missed only one League match the following campaign and two the season after that, playing almost exclusively as a skilful inside-left.

His personal highlight came in January 1933 when he scored the first hat-trick of his career against Chesterfield, and he was on the left wing when City gained one of their most famous FA Cup victories – a 3–1 triumph at Aston Villa in January 1935. He retired in 1936 after 477 senior matches, a combined total of 425 for the two Bradford clubs and 52 of them for Arsenal. He also scored 73 career goals, but years later he still regretted that City had failed to make the most of their promotion opportunities in the early 1930s.

Manager Jack Peart had built a fine team after taking over from Peter O'Rourke in 1930, and, writing in the *Yorkshire Sports* in 1949, Peel said 'We ought to have won the Second Division Championship in 1932–33 after being top at the halfway stage. We were a good team, but without real reserve strength. I was captain and Jack Peart used to ask me to come back in the afternoons to talk things over. We agreed we were playing as a tired team and that some of us ought to have a rest. I suggested going to market and buying two forwards and a half-back. Jack didn't disagree, but the club's policy was ruled by its finances and it was never done. I still think a little wise buying would have taken us up and that City would have been in the First Division today.'

After his football career was over, Peel became a successful businessman in Bradford. He died in January 1976.

Ces Podd

Date of birth: 7 August 1952

Bradford City record:
Appearances: League 502, FA Cup 30, League 34
Debut: 26 September 1970 v Chestefield

Also played for: Halifax Town, Scarborough
Managed: Nevis national side

No player has given Bradford City finer service than Ces Podd, who holds a special place in the club's history with a record number of League appearances – 502 in all – and he played a total of 574 League and Cup matches during a 14-year career at Valley Parade.

Podd, who was born on the Caribbean island of St Kitts, was one of the first black players to establish himself in League football. The slim right-back, who smiled his way through the game, conducted himself in a dignified manner even when he suffered verbal abuse and was a perfect role model on and off the field.

Years later, he said 'As far I was concerned colour did not apply, but I think it hindered my progress. I was 9st 6lb and 5ft 10in when I made my debut at City, but I looked bigger than I was because I was slim. In those days, back in the 1970s and early 1980s, there was a doubt about whether black players were physically able to play football and deal with the physical side of the game. That made me all the more determined. I wanted to win everything'.

Podd has seen the condition of black players improve considerably since he made his City debut in 1970. 'Every club in the Football League has got one black player, but where we are struggling is at the highest level and the management structure. Black talent is not being exploited. There should be more black managers and coaches – black people seem to have hit a barrier'.

It was largely due to City supporter Mick Illingworth that Podd became a professional footballer. Both were students at Bradford College of Art, where Podd was taking a two-year course in commercial design in advertising, and they used to play football at break time. Even though there was no college team, Mick Illingworth was impressed enough to write to Valley Parade suggesting that Podd be given a trial, and after completing his college course he was signed as a professional in August 1970 by manager Jimmy Wheeler.

Podd joined City two seasons after they had won promotion from the Fourth to the Third Division and made his debut in a 1–0 win at Chesterfield, making 28 appearances in his first season, but he played only nine matches the following season, which saw City relegated back to Division Four at a time of managerial changes. They began the season with Jimmy Wheeler in charge, but he was sacked after a bad start, which included a humiliating 7–1 defeat at Bristol Rovers. Former England World Cup hero Ray Wilson, then a youth coach at Valley Parade, took charge for two months and inspired a revival, but he didn't want the job and City turned to former Bolton defender Bryan Edwards, then assistant manager at Plymouth Argyle.

However, Podd gained a regular place the following season, making 40 League appearances, and was a regular for the next 12 years when his pace on the overlap and natural athleticism proved to be valuable assets.

Podd experienced highs and lows in his long Valley Parade career as City shuttled between the Third and Fourth Divisions, experiencing relegation in the 1971–72 and 1977–78 seasons and promotion in 1976–77 and 1981–82 and two of the highlights were famous Cup wins – a 1–0 win in the League Cup second-round first leg against Liverpool at Valley Parade in August 1980 – they lost the second leg 4–0 – and a 2–1 win at Norwich City in the FA Cup fifth round in February 1976, which set up a quarter-final tie against Southampton, which City lost 1–0.

Another highlight was his testimonial match at Valley Parade in March 1981. The fact that nearly all the leading black players in the League came to Bradford to support him speaks volumes about the respect Podd commanded.

He was an ever present when City gained promotion in 1981–82 under Roy McFarland and made 37 appearances the following season back in the Third Division, but his hold on the right-back spot began to loosen after that. Although he made 30 League appearances in 1983–84, significantly a young Greg Abbott played at right-back in the last 12 matches, and Podd was released after that campaign.

He joined Halifax Town, making 57 appearances for the Shay in two years before moving to Scarborough as assistant to recent Sheffield United manager Neil Warnock, and he helped them to win promotion to the Football League before retiring.

Since then, Podd has been involved with the Football in the Community programme at Leeds United, helping with coaching at the club's Academy and setting up coaching schemes around the Leeds area. He also spent two and a half years managing the national team on his home island of St Kitts and has worked for a football agency in Yorkshire as well as teaching salsa dancing.

Ivor Powell

Date of birth: 5 July 1916

Bradford City record:
Appearances: League 83, FA Cup 5
Goals: League 9
Debut: 23 August 1952 v Port Vale

Also played for: Queen's Park Rangers, Aston Villa, Port Vale
Managed: Port Vale, Bradford City, Carlisle United, Bath City

In the immediate post-war period it became a fashion among lower division clubs to appoint player-managers. The theory was that distinguished internationals would be able to pass on their considerable knowledge on and off the field while attracting larger crowds in the Third Division. So we had England international inside-forward Raich Carter as player-manager of Hull City, who regularly played in front of 30,000–plus crowds at Boothferry Park during his time in charge, his England teammate left-back George Hardwick at Oldham Athletic and Northern Ireland inside-forward Peter Doherty at Doncaster Rovers.

After parting company with David Steele in 1952, City followed the new trend and turned to Welsh international half-back Ivor Powell to be their player-manager, and what a dominant personality he turned out to be in his two years at the club, dictating the game in what we would now describe as a midfield role.

Powell, who celebrated his 91st birthday on 5 July 2007, has spent 75 years in professional football since signing for Queen's Park Rangers as a 17-year-old in 1933. Remarkably, he is still coaching at Bath University and now has a place in the *Guinness Book of Records* as the oldest working football coach, after being presented with the Guinness Certificate on his 90th birthday. He said 'I was pleased and very proud to receive the Guinness certificate. I've always had the aggression and determination to win and if I can keep that then I'll keep going. As long as I have my health then I will get pleasure from the game. I have enjoyed myself for all of these years, so why stop?'

He was working in the mines at the time he signed for Queen's Park Rangers, after being spotted playing for Bargoed, his local team in South Wales. However, his career at Queen's Park Rangers was interrupted by the war and he enlisted as an RAF physical training instructor and played as a guest for Blackpool where he struck up a long lasting friendship with Stanley Matthews, who was best man at his wedding.

He returned to Queen's Park Rangers in 1946, winning the first of four Welsh caps while at Queen's Park Rangers, and helped to inspire them to the Third Division South Championship in 1947–48, playing as an inside-forward. Such was his growing reputation that it was no surprise that he made the big breakthrough into the First Division midway through the following season. Aston Villa offered £17,500 – a record fee for both clubs – and Powell signed for them in December 1948. He was an ever present in his second season at Villa and was made captain. After making 79 League appearances with Villa and winning four more Welsh caps, Powell was offered the chance to go into management and took over as player-manager at Port Vale in 1951 before joining City the following year after the departure of David Steele.

There was an air of excitement at the appointment of a big-name player like Ivor Powell, but, despite some inspirational performances on the field, success eluded him. Even so, it was a pleasure to watch the forceful way he could dominate the game at Third Division level, even at his age – he was almost 36 when he joined City. What a player he must have been in his prime. Most of the passes went to him and he used to drive the team forward from a midfield position.

His first season ended in disappointment with City in 16th place, although a rousing end of season featuring four wins and only one defeat in the last seven matches offered encouragement for the following campaign. In the second half of the season those hopes were nearly fulfilled as City established a club record of nine consecutive wins – seven of them 1–0 victories. Sadly, after beating York City 1–0 at Valley Parade on 20 March, they failed to win a single one of their last 10 matches and finished fifth.

There was a promising start to the following campaign with six wins in the first 10 matches, but then Powell was carried off with knee ligament trouble in the 2–2 home draw against Wrexham on 15 September, and despite numerous attempts at a comeback he never played again. Without Powell's leadership on the field, the side slumped in form, and it was no surprise when he left the club the following February – 1955.

He became trainer coach at Leeds United in 1956 before returning to management with Carlisle United in May 1960, and he led them to promotion from the Fourth Division before becoming manager at Bath City in 1964. He settled in Bath and since 1973 he has worked as a football coach at the university, working with the university team, Team Bath. He is president of the team and helped them qualify for the FA Cup first round in 2002.

In 2004 he was inducted into the Welsh Sports Hall of Fame alongside other football legends such as John Charles and Ian Rush.

John Reid

Date of birth: 20 August 1932

Bradford City record:
Appearances: League 147, FA Cup 17, League Cup 3
Goals: League 32, FA Cup 2
Debut: 14 December 1957 v Carlisle United

Also played for: Kelso Rovers, Hamilton Academicals, Northampton Town, Luton Town, Torquay United, Rochdale
Managed: Market Rasen Town

Of all the Scottish players signed by Peter Jackson during his six-year spell at Bradford City manager, none turned out better than inside-forward John Reid, who joined City from Hamilton Academicals in December 1957 for £2,700, and what a bargain he turned out to be, even by the transfer values of the 1950s.

Reid's great strength was his speed over short distances, which gave him the time to display his skills, and he soon became a favourite with the Valley Parade crowd. He also scored his share of goals. He immediately established himself as a regular in the team at Valley Parade, playing at inside-left and forming an effective partnership with fellow inside-forward David Jackson.

He made 26 consecutive appearances to the end of the 1957-58 season, when City finished third in the final season of the Third Division North, scoring seven goals. At the end of the season, the top 12 clubs in the regional sections formed the new Third Division, the bottom 12 in each second section made up the new Fourth Division.

Reid missed 17 matches the following season as City finished in mid-table in the new national Third Division, but he made 41 League appearances in 1959-60, scoring eight goals, and played in every one of the eight FA Cup matches, scoring one of the goals when City beat First Division Everton in a memorable third-round tie at Valley Parade before they were knocked out of the Cup in a fifth-round replay by future League champions Burnley.

He played 40 League matches the following season when City were relegated and sacked manager Peter Jackson and, although he took his place in a new look team in the club's first season in the Fourth Division, he was on the move four months into the new campaign.

So, Reid left Valley Parade in November 1961 – six months after City's relegation – to join Northampton Town in a £5,000 deal, and he played a key role in their Third Division Championship triumph in 1962-63, but after scoring 14 goals in 85 League appearances at Northampton he moved to Luton Town in November 1963 for £13,000.

Reid couldn't save Luton from relegation to Division Four, but he was a popular player at Kenilworth Road, and the club made him captain. Unfortunately, they narrowly missed winning promotion at the first attempt, and after making 111 League appearances in two and a half years Luton sold Reid to Torquay in June 1966.

He spent only one season at Torquay before he returned north to finish his League career at Rochdale, having made 405 League appearances in a 10-year career in England and scoring 57 goals. His City record was 147 League appearances and 57 goals. He also played in 20 Cup matches, scoring twice.

Julian Rhodes

Bradford City record:
Director of Bradford City from 1997–present.
Chairman from 2004–07 when he became joint chairman with Mark Lawn.

Julian Rhodes is the modern saviour of Bradford City, the chairman and sole shareholder of the club since the last administration crisis in 2004. Without the investment provided by the Rhodes family and their tenacity and personal sacrifice in the face of seemingly insurmountable financial problems there would be no football club at Valley Parade. It's as simple as that.

So, when supporters complain or argue as they do about football issues like tactics or team selections, perhaps they should remember that there would be nothing to discuss if City had not survived the administration crises in 2002 and 2004. That the club emerged from these crises was down to the Rhodes family. Nor would City have enjoyed two seasons in the Premiership but for the investment in new players and the guarantees provided by current chairman Julian Rhodes and his father Professor David Rhodes.

They continued to help provide finance for the extensions and improvements to Valley Parade before guiding City through the perils of the two administrations when the future of the club hung by a thread. It was in January 1997 that Julian called chairman Geoffrey Richmond with a view to investing some money in the club. A meeting was arranged and the result was that Julian and his father bought 49 percent of the club's shares for a reported £3 million.

Julian Rhodes recalls that during the summer of 1998 Geoffrey Richmond thought the Division looked weak and City should have a crack at the Premiership. So, Geoffrey Richmond arranged for a firm of merchant bankers to give the club a £5 million facility to buy the players the club required for a promotion challenge. Geoffrey Richmond and David Rhodes were guarantors, but the Rhodes family put up £7.5 million shares from Professor Rhodes's high-tech company Filtronic to give cover.

City embarked on unprecedented expenditure in the transfer market as they bought three £1 million players, Lee Mills, Isaiah Rankin and Dean Windass, plus £600,000 for Gareth Whalley, and they won promotion to the Premiership.

The family made huge personal sacrifices so that League football could continue at Valley Parade. *The Pain and the Glory* book estimates that Professor Rhodes and Julian 'are credited with putting in £9 million in cash, with the Rhodes family also supplying about £20 million-worth of real security in the form of shares in their company, the family home of Professor and Mrs Rhodes and some hard cash'. They were paid back some £3 million from two dividends in 1999 and 2000, but the Rhodes family were still left 'massively out of pocket'.

Things went well in the first season in the Premiership, with City surviving on the last day of the campaign, but then came the so-called summer of madness and a spending spree on new players like Benito Carbone, Dan Petrescu and David Hopkin, who had huge wages. Relegation followed at the end of that season, and 12 months later the club slid into administration.

It was then that the Rhodes family made enormous personal sacrifices to help City to survive. For instance, Filtronic shares were used to secure a £5 million overdraft two months before the club went into administration in May 2002. More money was needed to make sure the Valley Parade staff were paid that summer, and over £1 million was still owed to the PFA. Part of this money came from Professor Rhodes's family home, plus more substantial cash payments and additional money from Professor Rhodes's pension provisions.

The club plunged into a new administration crisis in February 2004 and relegation followed three months later. Julian Rhodes provided the finance to make sure the club continued to the end of the season, but City's future was in jeopardy during an anxious summer. Ironically, the crisis deadline imposed by the administrators was reached on the day that new manager Colin Todd – he succeeded Bryan Robson – and the players resumed pre-season training not knowing whether they would have a future at Valley Parade. Fortunately, the Football League gave permission for City to start the new season while Julian Rhodes continued negotiations with key creditors in a bid to reach a 75 percent majority at a CVA meeting set for late August.

A new company, Bradford City Football Club Ltd, with Julian Rhodes as chairman, was formed. Since then, he has been looking for major investors to share the burden of running the football club, but without success. Former commercial manager Peter Etherington was promising to invest £2.5 million, but the deal fell through in July 2006.

In the meantime, the club have leased part of their offices to small businesses to bring in extra revenue and have signed a £2 million deal with a large catering firm and there was a further blow in 2007 when the club suffered their third relegation in six years when they dropped into League Two.

However, Rhodes, who had sacked manager Colin Todd four months before the end of the season appointed fans' favourite Stuart McCall to take his place and his search for a new investor ended when long-time supporter Mark Lawn joined the club as joint chairman after providing a reported seven-figure sum to clear off the debts.

Dean Richards

Date of birth: 9 June 1974

Bradford City record
Appearances: League 86, FA Cup 4, League Cup 7
Goals: League 4, FA Cup 1, League Cup 1
Debut: 26 October 1991 v AFC Bournemouth

Also played for: Wolverhampton Wanderers, Southampton, Tottenham Hotspur

Dean Richards was one of the best Bradford-born footballers of all time, but sadly his career was cut short by illness in 2003 when he was only 29. Richards, who went to Allerton Middle and Rhodesway Schools in Bradford, joined City as a youth trainee, signed as a full-time professional in 1992 and made his debut at 17, scoring in a 3-1 win at Bournemouth. He immediately impressed as a polished defender, who liked to play the ball constructively out of defence, and was clearly destined for higher-level football.

So, it was no surprise when he moved in March 1995 after making 86 League appearances at Valley Parade in one of chairman Geoffrey Richmond's multi-clause deals. It was expected that Richards would move into the Premiership, but the top clubs were clearly not convinced about his ability, and it was second-tier club Wolverhampton Wanderers who took the plunge, signing him first on loan and then in a transfer deal that initially was valued at £1.3 million but ultimately amounted to £1.8 million when various clauses took effect.

Richards made 122 League appearances in four years at Wolves and was at Molineux when City beat Wolves 3-2 in a thriller on a never-to-be-forgotten final day of the 1998-99 season to win promotion to the Premiership, and he was one of the first to go to the City dressing room and congratulate the team at the end of the match.

When his four-year contract was up, there was some speculation that he would return to Valley Parade and play Premiership football with his home-town club. However, Paul Jewell signed David Wetherall as his new central-defender that summer, and Richards got his wish to play in the top flight when he joined Southampton on a Bosman free transfer. He spent just over two years at Southampton, making 67 League appearances, first under Dave Jones, who later managed Wolves and Cardiff, and then under former England boss Glen Hoddle. When Hoddle moved to Tottenham Hotspur he signed Richards for Spurs in October 2001 for £8 million.

Richards, who made 73 League appearances for Spurs, played his last match in May 2003 when he was forced to announce his retirement after medical experts warned that his dizzy spells could lead to a brain haemorrhage if he continued to play. 'The analysis was that I was putting myself at risk if I continued playing,' he said, 'so the medical advice was to give up the game. The specialist said if I carried on playing I could have a brain haemorrhage. I wasn't worried about playing, but I have got a young family and to play on was a silly risk to take. I started young – I was playing first-team football at 17, and I did 13 years in the game so I have been lucky. I don't look back with any bitterness or resentment because football has given me a great life. I have been all over the world, and I have a great standard of living, so I have got to be grateful. I finished playing at the sort of club I aspired to playing for and I wouldn't have wanted to drop down the divisions.'

Although Richards is naturally disappointed that his career had to come to a sad and premature end, he said 'I look back on my career with a lot of pleasure. Every step I made was a forward step, and I still enjoy watching the game. You have to retire sometime – for me it was a couple of years too early – but worse things happened to players at 20 or 21. I see coaching as an option. I would like to get involved at academy or youth levels.' So, he is involved in a company in Spain and is now working as a coach at the Bradford City centre of excellence.

Geoffrey Richmond

Bradford City record:
Chairman from 1994–2002.
Also chairman of Scarborough.

Geoffrey Richmond was the most dominant and ambitious chairman in Bradford City's history, a man who gave Bradford City supporters a successful day out at Wembley, rebuilt three sides of Valley Parade and, above all, provided two seasons of Premiership football after a gap of 77 years from the top flight.

For the first six years of his eight-year chairmanship, everything went right for Geoffrey Richmond, before reckless overspending plunged the club into administration in 2002 and almost put City out of business. Less than two years later the club went back into administration and the subsequent financial constraints still dictate City's policy on and off the field.

Richmond, who made his millions from car stickers before taking over the ailing Ronson cigarette lighter company in Leeds and selling it for a reported £10 million, burst on to the Valley Parade scene in January 1994 when he and City chairman David Simpson engineered an unusual transfer arrangement. Richmond was Scarborough chairman and the two men agreed that Simpson would move to Scarborough and Richmond would take over at Valley Parade. He wanted a bigger stage, a club with more potential than Scarborough, and he saw City as that club.

City were struggling financially, and Richmond addressed that problem by loaning the club £2.3 million. He immediately made it clear that he would be a hands on chairman, controlling the club from the inside, ruthlessly clearing out staff he felt did not measure up to his standards, including manager Frank Stapleton, who left four months after Richmond arrived.

Richmond must have been frustrated by his first two years in charge, as City seemed to be stuck in mid-table. Stapleton was replaced by the experienced Lennie Lawrence, who gave way to his number two Chris Kamara in November 1995 – the first of Richmond's internal appointments.

Promotion looked unlikely when Kamara took over, but City ended the season with a flourish and booked their place in the Play-offs with a 3–2 win at Hull City in the last match of the season, before beating Blackpool in a two-leg semi-final Play-off tie to set up a visit to Wembley. To play at Wembley, twin towers and all, was a dream come true for City supporters, and 30,000 travelled from Bradford to watch them win promotion by beating Notts County 2–0 in the Play-off Final.

The following season Richmond again showed his ruthless streak, sacking Kamara halfway through the campaign and promoting his number two Paul Jewell, when some fans were clamouring for a so-called big-name manager.

Jewell proved to be an inspired appointment. In the summer of 1998 Richmond decided to go for promotion, and Jewell was given serious money to spend in the transfer market with funds secured by the Rhodes family, as explained earlier in this book, and three £1 million players – Lee Mills, Isaiah Rankin and Dean Windass – were signed as City made sure of promotion with an unforgettable 3–2 win at Wolves in the last match.

More money was spent in the close season, notably £1.4 million on Leeds United central-defender David Wetherall, and after a season of struggle against top-class opposition it was left to Wetherall to secure City's survival by scoring the winning goal against Liverpool in the last match of the season at Valley Parade.

Then came the fall-out with Jewell. The manager had complained about Richmond's interference in tactics, signing players and team selection, and there were more disagreements when they met at the end of the season about the players Jewell wanted to move on and the decision to enter the pre-season and InterToto Cup. It was then that Jewell decided to leave, and a month later he was appointed at Sheffield Wednesday.

Jewell's departure was a huge blow to the club, but Richmond moved on and appointed his assistant Chris Hutchings as a replacement before embarking on a spending spree, bringing in big-name players on huge salaries like Italian Benito Carbone on £40,000 a week, Dan Petrescu from Chelsea in a £1 million deal, David Hopkin, a club record £2.5 million signing from Leeds United, and Ashley Ward for £1.5 million from Blackburn Rovers, and City's wage bill rose to £14 million.

After a bad start to the season, Richmond sacked Hutchings in the first week in November and appointed former Hearts manager Jim Jefferies from Scotland as a replacement. The managerial change had no effect as City slid towards relegation. Jefferies lasted only 13 months before he too left the club, and Richmond appointed his sixth and last manager – Chesterfield boss Nicky Law.

Six months later, in May 2002, City went into administration for the first time. There followed an anxious four months as negotiations went on to try to secure the future of the club. Richmond and the Rhodes family tried separately to buy the club. Then Gordon Gibb, owner of the Flamingo Land fun park, offered to join Richmond, whereby Gibb would put up the money and Richmond would remain as chairman. Then there was a plan for the three of them to join forces, but finally Julian Rhodes and Gordon Gibb came together in a 50–50 deal, and Richmond found himself ousted by the Rhodes and Gibb families, who took control of the club in the August, just as the 2002–03 season was about to start.

Richmond was given guarantees that any liabilities in his name would be covered by the new partners, and so he was free of responsibilities. His eight-and-a-half-year spell at Valley Parade was at an end, and he said 'I went into my office on the following Monday and cleared my desk. As I drove away, I was in tears. It had been my life, and I have never been back since.'

Arthur Rigby

Date of birth: 1900
Died: March 1960

Bradford City record:
Appearances: League 121, FA Cup 6
Goals: League 21, FA Cup 1
Debut: 7 March 1921 v Aston Villa

Also played for: Crewe Alexandra (twice), Blackburn Rovers, Everton, Middlesbrough, Clapton Orient

Bradford City were busy in the transfer market in the early 1920s as the club tried to rejuvenate an ageing team. Overall, this transfer activity was not successful because not only were City relegated from the First Division in 1922, but they lost their Second Division status five years later despite constant changes in the team.

One of their better buys was outside-left Arthur Rigby, who went on to earn international recognition after he left Valley Parade in 1925.

Rigby, who was an electrician by trade, began his football career as a goalkeeper, but after a trial with Stockport County he developed as a winger and joined Crewe Alexandra – then a non-League club. The story goes that while he was in Crewe on business, City director Allan Welch took time off to sign Rigby for £1,200 and the player moved from non-League football into the First Division.

Rigby made 32 appearances for City in the top flight, but unfortunately the club were relegated after his first full season at Valley Parade. He was a regular for the next three seasons in the Second Division, but it was not until he was transferred to Blackburn Rovers for £2,500 in April 1925 that his career developed at the highest level.

He won five England caps and an FA Cup-winners' medal during his career at Ewood Park and also represented the Football League. After making 156 League appearances for Blackburn and scoring 42 goals – a good record for a winger – he was transferred to Everton in November 1929, and in the 1930–31 season he won a Second Division Championship medal with the Toffees.

Rigby later played for Middlesbrough, whom he joined at the end of the 1931–32 season, and Clapton Orient, now Leyton Orient, at the start of the 1933–34 campaign. He rejoined Crewe two years later and retired from there in 1937, having made 467 League appearances and scored 108 goals, including 121 and 21 goals with City.

George Robinson

Date of birth: 1878
Died: March 1945

Bradford City record:
Appearances: League 343, FA Cup 34
Goals: League 16, FA Cup 3
Debut: 1 September 1903 v Grimsby Town

Also played for: Notts Jardines, Newark, Nottingham Forest

George Robinson played in City's first ever Football League match at Grimsby in 1903 and became one of their best signings. Robinson, who was born at Basford in Nottinghamshire, began his professional career with Nottingham Forest after playing with Notts Jardines and Newark. He made his League debut against Bolton Wanderers in April 1899 and made 63 appearances for Forest before becoming one of City's first signings in June 1903 – one month after the club were elected to the Football League.

The right-half-back played in City's first ever Football League match at Grimsby, and in his 12-year career he set what was then a club record of 343 League appearances, while also playing in 34 FA Cup matches. That appearance record stood until 1972 when it was beaten by Bruce Stowell.

Robinson was so consistent that he was an ever present in three seasons, including City's first two campaigns when they were trying to establish themselves as a League club. He captained City when they won the Second Division Championship in 1907-08, and his consistency continued to be a shining light as the club began to establish themselves in the First Division.

Robinson made 34 League appearances in City's first season in the top flight, and he was an ever present the following season. He missed 11 matches in 1910-11 when City achieved their highest ever League placing – fifth in the top flight – but played in all seven FA Cup matches as City won the FA Cup by beating Newcastle United in the Final after a replay. In fact, Robinson was one of only two Englishmen in the side that beat Newcastle to bring the coveted trophy to Bradford.

Robinson played in 25 League matches the following season and five of their FA Cup matches as they tried in vain to retain the Cup. They reached the quarter-final before they were beaten by eventual winners Barnsley after two replays.

His appearances gradually began to tail off after that – he played in 19 League matches in 1912-13 and started the following season well, missing only one of the first 19 matches, but he made only five appearances in the second half of the campaign.

He lost his place in 1914-15, the last season before League football was suspended because of the war, playing only three times as Joe Hargreaves gradually took over the right-half spot.

By that time he was 36 and his playing career ended after he made one wartime appearance, but he remained at Valley Parade as first-team trainer until 1922, when the club lost their First Division status.

George Robinson, front row far right, in the Bradford team of 1908-09.

Abe Rosenthal

Date of birth: 12 October 1921
Died: February 1986

Bradford City record:
Appearances: League 108, FA Cup 3
Goals: League 43
Debut: 24 May 1947 v Doncaster Rovers

Also played for: Tranmere Rovers (three spells)

Abe Rosenthal was a roly poly character with a smile on his face, who played football for fun – literally. The Liverpool born inside-forward, who unusually had three separate spells at Bradford City and Tranmere Rovers during his career, once revealed that nearly all his part-time wages of £9 he earned at Tranmere went in tax because his lollipop business was so successful. The revelation came after Rosenthal, who weighed 14st, had scored the winning goal for Tranmere in a FA Cup third-round tie at Huddersfield Town in January 1952.

As the second biggest lollipop manufacturer in the country, he employed more people than the club that paid his wages. At that time Abe had business interests in Bradford and Manchester – Roscana Lollipops – and employed 25 people in the winter and more than 50 in the summer. He told the newspapers 'I just play for the fun of the game now, but I meant to make it my career when I signed on for Tranmere in 1938 as a boy of 17.'

Abe went into the lollipop business with his brother-in-law after the war and played part-time for City and Tranmere, and on hot days during pre-season training he was known to supply the players with ice creams.

Like many players of his generation, Rosenthal's career was badly disrupted by the war, taking out seven seasons in all, so, although he was one month short of his 18th birthday when war was declared in September 1939, he was almost 25 when League football resumed in August 1946.

By this time he was establishing the lollipop business at the top of Valley Parade, literally within a stone's throw of City's ground, so it was natural that he should want to move to the Bantams and did so for the first time in April 1947, the first season after the war ended. City paid a four-figure fee for the player, setting in motion an extraordinary series of transfers between City and Tranmere over the following 10 years as Rosenthal crises crossed between the two Third Division North clubs playing as a part-time professional. Even when he played with Tranmere, he would train at Valley Parade during the week and travel to the Wirral for weekend matches.

He was a regular in the 1947–48 season, scoring 11 goals in 33 League matches, but he struggled to establish a regular place the season after that under new manager David Steele and after making eight appearances he was on his way back to Tranmere in February 1949 after City agreed to cancel his contract.

Rosenthal returned to Valley Parade in July 1952 on a free transfer under new manager Ivor Powell, and the next two seasons were the best of his City career. He scored 17 goals in 37 matches in his first season and was leading scorer with 15 goals in 26 matches when City finished fifth in the Third Division North in 1953–54.

Abe went back to Tranmere for the third and last time in July 1954 on a free transfer after City again agreed to cancel his contract. He returned to City under new manager Peter Jackson in the summer of 1955 but made just one appearance before retiring from professional football. He made 108 League appearances for City, scoring 43 goals, and 117 appearances for Tranmere, scoring 35 goals.

Rosenthal's build meant he was slow, especially by modern standards, but he possessed delightful skills on the ball, and he liked nothing better than beating his opponent more than once. While that might have delighted the crowd, it often frustrated his manager, but then football was fun to Abe, and he always played with a smile on his face.

One abiding memory of him came in a West Riding Senior Cup Final between City and Park Avenue at Valley Parade on a warm spring evening in May 1953, the Friday after the season had ended. There was a lot of local pride at stake and the match attracted a crowd of 14,555. Park Avenue won 3–2 after extra-time and one of the City goals was scored in extraordinary fashion by Abe. Sitting on the ground with his back to goal after a goalmouth scramble, he stuck out his foot as the ball was returned into the goalmouth and it flew over his head and into the net. The goal not only gave him pleasure, but he could also see the funny side of it. The broad grin on his face as he turned to the crowd on the Spion Kop summed up his approach to the game. It is unlikely we will ever see a player like him in today's game.

Rosenthal wanted to play as an amateur with Salts when his League career was over, but the Football Association turned down his request to change status from professional to amateur because they feared it would create a precedent. Happily, that doesn't apply now because there is no distinction between amateur and professional, and it is quite common for a full-time professionals to go and play for local clubs, who, of course, can offer attractive part-time terms.

Abe eventually returned to his home city of Liverpool and died there in tragic circumstances in February 1986. Abe disturbed two youths inside his home at Speke, chased them down the street and then collapsed and died from a heart attack.

Lee Sinnott

Date of birth: 12 July 1965

Bradford City record:
Appearances: League 214, FA Cup 11, League Cup 21
Goals: League 7
Debut: 15 August 1987 v Swindon Town

Also played for: Walsall, Watford, Crystal Palace, Huddersfield Town, Oldham Athletic
Managed: Farsley Celtic

Lee Sinnott was Bradford City's record signing when he joined the club for £130,000 from Watford in the 1987 close season. Having established themselves in the Second Division after winning the Third Division Championship two years earlier, the club were ready for a serious promotion challenge. So, manager Terry Dolan prepared for his first full season in charge by making two big signings – Sinnott, a tall 23-year-old central defender with pace, and experienced goalkeeper Paul Tomlinson from Sheffield United.

Unfortunately for City, their promotion bid failed, for, after being in a strong position all season, they faltered at the end, losing their chance of an automatic promotion place when they were beaten in their last two matches against Aston Villa and Ipswich before losing to Middlesbrough in the Play-off semi-final.

Sinnott, who was an England youth international and later played one match for England Under-21s, began his career in his native Midlands with Walsall. He made 40 League appearances for them before joining Watford, for whom he played in the 1984 FA Cup Final against Liverpool when still only 18.

He had three spells at Valley Parade, leaving for Crystal Palace in 1991 after four years before returning two years later. Twelve months after that he was on the move again – this time to Huddersfield Town with Lee Duxbury in a deal that saw defender Graham Mitchell join City. He then had a brief spell on loan at the end of the 1997–98 season, just after Paul Jewell took over as manager.

Sinnott, who is a successful manager of Farsley Celtic, having guided them from the Unibond Premier League to Conference North and The Conference in successive seasons, played 214 League matches in his three spells at Valley Parade, but he regards his first spell as the best.

Sinnott said 'I came to Bradford after four years at Watford – four crucial years in my career. I worked with Steve Harrison, John Ward and Graham Taylor at Watford, and they taught me a lot as a defender. Coming to Bradford was the right move for me and the correct decision. I was 23 when I joined Bradford and I had a wonderful time. It was very enjoyable.

'In what I call the nearly season, when we were beaten by Middlesbrough in the Second Division Play-offs, it was an amazing feat to get so far considering the size of the squad. We operated with only 16 or 17 players. Terry Dolan did extremely well – we just ran out of steam at the end and John Hendrie's suspension, which meant he missed the last match of the season, cost us.'

To the commonly held view that City would have gained promotion if they had signed the two players that Dolan wanted to sign just before the transfer deadline, Sinnott said 'You cannot guarantee it would have made the difference, but it would have helped. For instance, we only had 14 fit players for the Play-off semi-final second leg at Middlesbrough.'

Apart from that season, other highlights for Sinnott came in the following campaign when City beat Everton 3–1 at home in the League Cup and Tottenham Hotspur 1–0 at home in the FA Cup. 'Valley Parade wasn't as developed as it is now,' he said, 'but it generated a fantastic atmosphere especially at a night game, and Everton were one of the top clubs in the country at that time.'

Sinnott was transferred to Crystal Palace in the summer of 1991 for £350,000. 'I had had three opportunities to move before then,' he said. 'The club informed me when clubs made inquiries, but I was still enjoying my football at Valley Parade so I stayed. In hindsight, maybe it was not a good move to go to Palace. I had the choice between Palace and Southampton. In fact, I was going to Southampton when Palace heard about it.

'I came back to Valley Parade for £50,000 before being sold a year later to Huddersfield Town along with Lee Duxbury – the club obviously needed the money.'

Geoff Smith

Date of birth: 14 March 1928

Bradford City record:
Appearances: League 253, FA Cup 17
Debut: 17 January 1953 v Scunthorpe United

Also played for: Rossendale, Nelson

Geoff Smith swapped lorry driving for full-time football, and he went on to play 270 League and FA Cup games in seven seasons for Bradford City during the 1950s. Consistency was a byword in Smith's career, but his introduction to League football was not straightforward. Born in the Cottingley area of Bingley, he was playing for Keighley Central Youth Club when City offered him a trial in 1948, but nothing came of it and he joined Nelson in the Lancashire Combination before playing for Rossendale United in the same League.

In December 1952 City invited him back, and after a further trial he signed as an amateur. He was still an amateur when player-manager Ivor Powell gave him his League debut at Scunthorpe United in January 1953, replacing Brendan McManus. He stayed in the side – making 19 consecutive appearances – until the end of the season, and in July 1953 he became a part-time professional, becoming full-time two years later.

Although Smith had been first choice in the second half of the season, Powell signed a new goalkeeper for the new campaign, the experienced 32-year-old Graham Gooch from Preston as McManus left to join non-League Frickley.

Gooch played in the first half of the season before Smith re-claimed his place in the side at the end of November. Such was Smith's consistency that Gooch played only two more matches towards the end of the season before leaving in the summer to join Watford.

That left the way clear for Smith, and he embarked a run of 200 consecutive League appearances, which included four seasons as an ever present. The run began with the last match of the 1953-54 season at home to Gateshead and ended at Reading in October 1958. He made 26 League appearances that season before retiring. Smith also went 18 matches in season 1957-58 without conceding a goal and kept 70 'clean sheets' during his career.

Recalling his early days in football, Smith said 'When I played at Nelson I travelled by bus from my home at Keighley. I went to Nelson with my brother Jack, who had played at Leeds United, but had been released when Major Buckley took over at Elland Road.

'I stayed at Nelson for about three years, but they couldn't afford to pay me and I gave up the game. Then Rossendale, who played in the same League but in the Second Division, took me on and I played with them for a couple of years. It was a difficult journey by bus so I bought a motor bike, but then they could not afford to pay either so, again, I packed up the game.

'Then, the City player manager Ivor Powell wanted a goalkeeper and I was approached by a friend, Roy Brook, who was in the second team at Valley Parade. Ivor Powell asked me to go for a trial and I played my first reserve game at Gainsborough Trinity in the Midland League followed by a home match against Notts County.

'The first team goalkeeper Brendan McManus was having a rough time so I was put in the first team at Scunthorpe.

'I was an amateur when I got into the first team at City, still working as a wagon driver, but the club didn't want me travelling all over the country so they gave me a job looking after the ground.

'I gave up the lorry driving job, which earned me £4 10s (£4.50), for a 48-hour week for £10 a week – the maximum wage throughout the Football League was £12 – plus a £4 bonus for a win as a footballer, which was a good deal.'

Smith has many memories of his first manager at Valley Parade, former Welsh international half-back Ivor Powell. 'He was a good player, but a hard task master and used to sort you out on the field if there was anything wrong. Unfortunately, he expected you to be the same standard as him.'

Powell was famous for his malapropisms and on one occasion he asked the players to 'amalgamate' at Forster Square Station for an away trip.

Jimmy Speirs

Date of birth: 1886
Died: 1917

Bradford City record:
Appearances: League 86, FA Cup 10
Goals: League 29, FA Cup 4
Debut: 1 September 1909 v Manchester United

Also played for: Glasgow Rangers, Clyde

Captain Jimmy Speirs carved himself a special place in Bradford City's history when he scored the only goal in the 1911 FA Cup Final replay.

A goalscoring inside-forward, Speirs enjoyed an impressive football career starting with Glasgow Rangers and Clyde in his native Scotland before moving to England to play for City and Leeds City (later Leeds United), but football was only part of Jimmy Speirs remarkable life. For, he was also a war hero, being awarded the Military Medal 'for bravery in the field' before, like so many of his generation, he died on Flanders fields in 1917 at the age of 31, leaving a wife and two children aged nine and five.

Speirs began his football career in 1905 with Maryhill in the Glasgow Junior League before being offered his breakthrough into the Scottish League at Glasgow Rangers. He spent three years at Ibrox, scoring 29 League and Cup goals in 62 matches, and was joint top scorer in 1906–07 with 13 League goals, but it was not a particularly successful spell in Rangers' illustrious history, as they finished fourth in Speirs's first season and third in the other two without ever threatening to win the Scottish Championship. Then, as now, the main issue in Scotland was the rivalry between Rangers and Celtic and who would win the title. Unfortunately for Speirs, Celtic won the Championship in all three seasons he spent at Ibrox. Nor was there any joy in the Cup, although Speirs scored a hat-trick in a 7–1 first-round win over Second Division Arthurlie in the Scottish Cup in his first season. So, the only medal Speirs won in his time at Rangers was the Glasgow Merchants Charity Cup, also in his first season. He scored twice in a 5–3 win over Celtic in the semi-final and twice in the victory over Queen's Park in the Final.

Speirs moved to another Glasgow club, Clyde, who were also in the First Division, in 1908 and played one season there, scoring 10 goals in 20 matches, and helping them to finish third and reach the Scottish Cup semi-final, when they were beaten by Celtic after a replay.

Then came his big move to England. Speirs signed for City in the summer of 1909 for their second season in the First Division, as manager Peter O'Rourke began to strengthen his side after the club narrowly escaped relegation in their first season in the top flight. Interestingly, England international Dickie Bond also joined City that close season.

The Scot was a huge success in his first season, being an ever present with 38 League appearances and scoring six goals.

However, it was in the following season that he wrote his place in City's history. He scored seven goals in 25 League appearances as City achieved their highest-ever placing – fifth in the top division, seven points behind champions Manchester United, but it was the FA Cup that provided Speirs with his finest hour.

Speirs, then 25, was not only captain of the side, but he scored the winning goal in the Cup Final replay against Newcastle at Old Trafford and proudly received the coveted trophy before leading the victory parade in a packed Bradford city centre later that evening. He played only 10 times in the League the following season, scoring seven goals, and moved to Leeds City for £1,400 – a sizeable fee at a time when the average wage was £2 a week and top players earned £4 – in December 1912, just 18 months after lifting the FA Cup for City. In three and a half seasons at Valley Parade Speirs scored 33 goals in 96 League and Cup matches.

League football continued in the first year of the war before being suspended in May 1915, when it was realised that there would be no early end to the hostilities. Speirs scored 10 goals in 25 appearances in what proved to be his last season.

After the season was over, Speirs returned home to Glasgow and volunteered to enlist in the Queen's Own Cameron Highlanders. Conscription was still a year away, and Speirs would have been exempt on the grounds of being married with two young children, but he still volunteered to join the war. He was promoted to lance corporal while training at Inverness, and, following heavy casualties on the front, men from the reserve battalion were posted overseas. So in March 1916 Speirs left Scotland to go to France, and four months later he was promoted to corporal.

He wounded his elbow, and in May 1917 he was awarded the Military Medal for 'bravery in the field', although no details were given. Promotions continued for Speirs as the leadership skills he showed on the football field were recognised by the military authorities, and in June 1917 he was promoted to sergeant.

Speirs came home on leave in the July, but he returned to France and was killed in the Battle of Passchendaele on or about 20 August.

Derek Stokes

Date of birth: 13 September 1939

Bradford City record:
Appearances: League 126, FA Cup 13, League Cup 2
Goals: League 55, FA Cup 11
Debut: 14 September 1957 v Crewe Alexandra

Also played for: Snydale, Huddersfield Town, Dundalk

Over an eight-year period in the late 1950s and early 1960s, Bradford City managed to produce no fewer than four outstanding, goalscoring centre-forwards, among them Derek Stokes, whose remarkable season in which he scored 35 League and FA Cup goals in 45 appearances in 1959-60 led to a big-money transfer to local rivals Huddersfield Town.

Stokes joined City as an amateur from West Yorkshire League side Snydale in May 1956 and signed part-time professional forms the following April before becoming a full-time professional in January 1958. He began his career as an outside-left, but, when manager Peter Jackson switched him to centre-forward after John McCole was transferred to Leeds United in September 1959, not even he could have imagined how successful that move would become.

Stokes had shown his goalscoring ability the season before when he scored 15 goals in 45 League appearances and one in the FA Cup despite playing every game on the wing, but his career took off in a big way the following season when he scored 25 goals in 37 League matches and 10 in City's eight Cup games.

That was the memorable season when City reached the fifth round before crashing out 5-0 in a replay against future League champions Burnley at Turf Moor after City had let a 2-0 lead slip in the first match at Valley Parade. Unfortunately for City, Stokes missed the last nine matches through injury, and it was a sign of how much they depended on him that they scored only seven goals in that spell without him.

Stokes enjoyed a successful six years in the higher division with Huddersfield, scoring 65 goals in 153 League matches – slightly over one goal in three appearances before returning to City in January 1966. However, those who hoped that he could repeat the goalscoring record of his first spell were to be disappointed, and after scoring 11 goals in 32 appearances he left after 11 months at Valley Parade to pursue his career in the Republic of Ireland, where he played for Dundalk in European competition.

Stokes, who now lives in retirement near Lyme Regis in Dorset, recalls scoring twice in a 2-2 draw at Crewe on 14 September 1957, the day after his 18th birthday, but many of his happy memories of Valley Parade concern the Cup run of 1959-60 and the two big matches against First Division opponents – Everton and Burnley. Stokes scored one of the goals in the 3-0 win over Everton and another goal as City went 2-0 ahead against Burnley before having to settle for a 2-2 draw after the visitors' stoppage time equaliser.

He said 'We were very unlucky at home to Burnley. The referee must have played 10 minutes over time, when Burnley scored their equaliser. In fact, everyone was shouting "have you lost your watch?" The equaliser came from a free kick, which could have been cleared. Tom Flockett could have cleared the ball. He tried to take the ball off their player, but he didn't and when the cross came in the ball went into the net off Ray Pointer's knee. Then we got hammered in the replay.

'We had some good players at Valley Parade at that time. I particularly remember John McCole – he had so much talent – the Jackson twins, Peter and David, Bobby Webb, Martin Bakes, Jim Lawlor, David Boyle – all good players.

'In the summer of 1960, I got a good move to Huddersfield Town, who were then in the Second Division, and I was top scorer for five years so I didn't do too bad, but it was more difficult to score in the higher division – I played up front with Les Massie and Len White.

'I started my National Service in the RAF just after I signed for Huddersfield and that took two years out of my career, which was a shame, but I played four times for the England Under-23 team.

'I went back to City in 1966, but it didn't work out too well so when our centre-half Alan Fox went to Ireland to become player-manager of Dundalk he asked me to go with him. We won the League and Cup in the first year I was there and we played in the old Fairs Cup for three years. We played the Hungarian team Vasas, and I also remember playing Rangers and Liverpool.

'After three years in Ireland I went back to England and managed Fryston Colliery Welfare in the West Yorkshire League and took them into the Yorkshire League. Since then I have been steward at Woodhills Golf Club near Leeds and Ormskirk in Lancashire.

'We enjoyed playing football in my day more, I think, than the players do now. It wasn't such a big business then.'

Charlie Storer

Date of birth: 1891
Died: 9 May 1956

Bradford City record:
Appearances: League 208, FA Cup 13
Goals: League 13
Debut: 15 March 1913 v Manchester City

Also played for: Gresley Rovers, Hartlepool United

Charlie Storer was a member of the famous half-back line of Hargreaves-Storer-Duckett, which was a feature of Bradford City's team in the seasons after World War One. However, Storer began his career as a centre-forward – and also nearly joined First Division rivals Chelsea instead of City. He played as a centre-forward in junior football in his native Leicestershire when he joined City as a 21-year-old in March 1913 and in the early part of his Valley Parade career.

However, after regular centre-half Bob Torrance – one of City's FA Cup Final heroes – tragically lost his life in World War One, Storer took his place and remained there until he left to sign for Hartlepool in 1924.

Storer, who was a miner at Whitwick in the Leicestershire coalfield, began his football career playing centre-forward for his home village team, Ibstock Albion, in the Leicestershire Senior League. He later moved to Gresley Rovers where some big clubs, including City, spotted him.

Recalling his early days in a *Yorkshire Sports* article more than 30 years later, Storer said it was 'touch and go' whether he became a City player. 'I nearly went to Chelsea after I'd got a lot of goals, but they took our right-back instead of me', he recalled. 'Then I heard afterwards that Peter O'Rourke (City manager) had watched me three times and John Lucas, then a City director, also had a look at me before both of them asked me how I'd like the idea of a move to Bradford.

'It came to be a question of terms. I was a coal miner at the time, and Peter asked me what my pay was in the pits. When I told him it was 30s (£1.50 in today's money) a week he said "Suppose we give you £2 and make it £4 when you are in the first team." I jumped at the chance and I thought I was a millionaire when I took that turning point in my career and came to Bradford in 1913. It made me feel that football fame wasn't far away and that I'd soon jump to the top.

'Sure enough within a week or two after my move and after I'd had only two games in the second team, I found myself in First Division football as an inside-left against Manchester City and it still remains as the biggest moment of my career. But, as it turned out, I had a long way to go and a long time to wait before I really got established in the top class. City soon moved me back to the middle, and I was a forward right up to the war starting, but I never fell in love with the position and I can't say I really pulled up any trees when my job was concerned chiefly with getting goals'.

Storer recalled that he became a centre-half by accident. He had gone back to work in the mines at Whitwick when war broke out and guested for Leicester Fosse (now Leicester City) in season 1915-16. They played at Grimsby, but two players couldn't play because of work, the trainer forgot the skip containing the kit when they changed trains at Woodhouse near Sheffield and so when they arrived at Grimsby they were two players short and with no kit.

He added 'One of the re-arrangements that had to be made in our team caused me to be switched to centre-half where I had never played before, Teddy King, our regular in that position, being one of those who had had to cry off. We won the match 3-1, but we never scored a goal. Grimsby lent us not only boots, jerseys, shorts and socks, but also an inside-right and an inside-left. Both of them scored and the Grimsby left-back put one past his own goalkeeper for good measure. That was what I call being really hospitable to visitors. I must have had a good game that day because I stayed at centre-half and when the war was over City made me the successor to poor Bob Torrance'.

Storer made his debut in a 2-1 home win against Manchester City on 15 March 1913 and played in the remaining 11 matches of that season all at inside-left and scored seven goals in 27 League matches the following season, all but three of them at centre-forward as Frank O'Rourke gradually faded from the first-team scene. Seven more appearances followed in 1914-15 – the last season before League football was suspended because of the war, and after the hostilities Storer reappeared as a centre-half.

So, he took part in City's last three seasons in the First Division, missing only one match in 1919-20, and after suffering the heartache of relegation in 1922 he played two seasons in Division Two before joining Hartlepool for what was his last season. He made 35 appearances in a side that narrowly missed having to seek re-election to Division Three North, but after retiring from the professional game he continued to play local football until World War Two.

In eight peacetime seasons at Valley Parade either side of the war, he made 208 League and 13 FA Cup appearances, scoring 13 goals. Storer stayed in Bradford, becoming licensee of the Bradford Arms in Manningham Lane, a few hundred yards from Valley Parade, and when he retired in 1956, after 32 years there, his son Charles Junior held the licence until 1986.

Bruce Stowell

Date of birth: 20 September 1941

Bradford City record:
Appearances: League 401, FA Cup 16, League Cup 20
Goals: League 16, FA Cup 1, League Cup 1
Debut: 16 April 1960 v Colchester United

Also played for: Rotherham United
Managed: Newcastle Breakers, Brisbane Strikers

Bradford-born Bruce Stowell broke Bradford City's appearance record during a 14-year spell at Valley Parade, before developing an impressive coaching career in Australia. Few players have given better service than the hard working, strong tackling half-back and inside-forward, who made 401 League appearances for the club and played in 36 Cup matches, scoring 18 goals.

A contemporary of Bobby Ham – both attended Grange School in Bradford – Stowell captained Bradford Boys in their annual and prestigious fixture against Glasgow Boys and played as an amateur for Leeds United before joining City, also as an amateur, in May 1958. He turned part-time professional in December that year, but did not turn full-time professional until June 1967, when he took over the captaincy.

Stowell made his debut at right-half on Easter Saturday 16 April 1960 in a 2-1 defeat at Colchester, as the season fell away badly following the club's memorable FA Cup run that saw them reach the fifth round in those never to be forgotten matches against Burnley.

He played four matches that season and nine the following season, when City were relegated to the Fourth Division, but began to establish a regular place in the side in the second half of the following season, scoring six goals in 24 appearances, most of them at inside-right, as the club narrowly failed to gain promotion back to the Third Division by one place.

Seventeen appearances followed the next season when City had to apply for re-election, but he played 29 times in 1963-64 when City again failed to gain promotion by one place. From then he won a permanent place in the team, missing only four matches in 1964-65, seven in 1965-66, six in 1966-67 and four in 1967-68, when City again finished in fifth place – one place away from promotion.

Undoubtedly, the highlight of Stowell's career came the following season when he led City to promotion in fourth place after a superb second half of the season, when they lost only one of their last 23 matches and made certain of fourth place by winning 3-1 in a memorable final match at Darlington.

The following season Stowell played a key role in one of the best post-war Cup matches at Valley Parade. City drew Tottenham Hotspur in the FA Cup third round in January 1970, and Spurs, who included famous names like Jimmy Greaves, Alan Gilzean, Mike England, Alan Mullery, Steve Perryman and Pat Jennings in their team, went 2-0 in front early in the game through Greaves and Roger Morgan. However, City hit back to draw level before half-time, with Stowell scoring the equaliser, and 2-2 was the final score. Unfortunately for City, they crashed 5-0 in the replay.

Stowell missed only one match in the promotion season and broke George Robinson's 55-year-old club record when he made his 344th League appearance in a home match against Walsall in October 1970. He continued to play regularly after promotion, missing only five League matches in 1969-70 and playing 38 the following season and 32 in 1971-72, when the club were relegated back to Division Four.

However, Stowell surprisingly left City that summer, joining Rotherham United on a free transfer, but he played only 16 matches for Rotherham before accepting a two-year contract with the Sydney club Pan Hellenic and left for Australia with his family in May 1973. The move to Australia opened a remarkable career in playing, coaching and management at club and national level. He received the Rothmans Gold Award for Player of the Year in 1976 and was Queensland State technical director of coaching for eight years between 1983 and 1991, and then he enjoyed two-year spells as manager and coach of National Soccer League clubs Newcastle Breakers and Brisbane Strikers.

After one year as North Queensland technical director of coaching, he was appointed head coach of Johor FC in Malaysia in 1999, but a year later he took up his current work as head coach of Queensland Academy of Sport Men's Football Program in 2001. Stowell has also made a significant impact as a coach at a national level. He was appointed Australian staff coach in 1978 and was national Under-16s coach, leading them to the World Cup quarter-finals in China in 1985 and again in Canada in 1987, when he received the Sport Australia award as coach for outstanding performance as well as the Team of the Year award. He was assistant national coach at Under-17 level for the World Cup qualifiers in 2003 and 2005 and was also certified FIFA instructor at the Oceania International Academy in 1985 and was the principal coach of their senior coaching academy.

Paul Tomlinson

Date of birth: 4 February 1965

Bradford City record:
Appearances: League 293, FA Cup 15, League Cup 28
Debut: 15 August 1987 v Swindon Town

Also played for: Sheffield United, Birmingham City (loan)

Paul Tomlinson was a significant signing when he joined Bradford City in the 1987 close season from Sheffield United in a £47,000 deal. Terry Dolan, preparing for his first full season as manager, clearly wanted a new goalkeeper and chose 22-year-old Tomlinson, who had struggled to command a regular place at Bramall Lane. He arrived at Valley Parade, having played 37 League matches for the Blades during the previous three years and having also played 11 matches while on loan to Birmingham City. So, he was looking for regular first-team football and City gave him that.

Defender Lee Sinnott – a record £130,000 signing when he joined the club from Watford that summer – was the other key recruit as Dolan put together a team to make a serious promotion challenge, which ended in heartache as City were beaten in the Play-offs.

The burly, 6ft-plus Tomlinson, who replaced Peter Litchfield, was ideally built for a goalkeeper and was to prove to be City's first choice for the next eight years. By the time he left the club he had made 293 League appearances, more than any other 'keeper in Bradford's 104-year history.

Tomlinson missed only two matches in his first season as City were edged out of an automatic promotion place by losing their last match of the season – 3-2 at home to Ipswich – before Middlesbrough beat them in the Play-offs. They also reached the fifth round of the FA Cup before losing 3-0 at Portsmouth and the quarter-finals of the League Cup before Luton beat them 2-0 at Kenilworth Road.

The next three seasons were periods of big changes at Valley Parade with two new managers and relegation back to the third tier of League football, but Tomlinson kept his regular place in the side. He made 38 League appearances in 1988-89, when Dolan lost his job, and was replaced by former City coach, then Swansea manager, Terry Yorath. City were too inconsistent to make a promotion challenge that season, but Dolan led them to the fourth round of the FA Cup after beating Tottenham Hotspur 1-0 at home in a memorable third-round tie, only to lose to Hull City in the fourth round. He also led them to the quarter-finals of the League Cup for the second season in a row after a superb 3-1 home win over Everton, only to lose 1-0 at home to Bristol City before he was sacked.

Tomlinson played 41 League matches in 1989-90 as Yorath was replaced by former Millwall manager John Docherty and City were relegated only two seasons after their failed promotion bid. His consistency continued to be a strong feature as he missed only three matches in 1990-91 – Docherty's only full season – and then missed only one match the following campaign when player-manager Frank Stapleton arrived at Valley Parade as Docherty's replacement.

Back problems restricted Tomlinson's appearances to 24 matches in 1992-93 and 23 in 1993-94, but he recovered to play 37 matches under new manager Lennie Lawrence in 1994-95, which proved to be his last season at Valley Parade.

Tomlinson rejected City's offer of a new contract at the end of that season as Lawrence brought in a new 'keeper, Gavin Ward from Leicester City. Eventually, he became a free agent, but he never played League football again and it seemed a shame that he had to retire at only 30 years old.

It also seemed ironic that having gone through some barren seasons in the Third Division he should miss out on some good times at Valley Parade, for in the new season City gained promotion through the Play-offs, beating Notts County in the Final at Wembley, and three years later they won promotion to the Premiership.

However, Tomlinson said 'I rejected a new contract because, towards the end of the season Lennie Lawrence first offered me a new two-year contract, which would have taken me to my testimonial, but then the club offered a one-year deal on the same money. I saw that as the club going back on their word, especially as I had done eight years there. I didn't need to be treated like that so I decided to pack in the game. I was going to sign for Chesterfield and I went training there, but my back wasn't up to it.'

Jack Tordoff

Bradford City record:
Director 1975–78 and 1983–90.
Chairman 1987–90.
Life president from 1990.

No businessman has given Bradford City more sustained support over a longer period than Jack Tordoff. Founder of the motor dealer firm JCT 600, Jack Tordoff is one of the most successful businessmen in the north of England, and he has generously used his considerable resources to support his home city of Bradford. He has had two spells as director at Valley Parade, including two years as chairman, and continues to support the football club, but in more recent years Bradford Bulls Rugby League club, Bradford & Bingley Rugby Union club and Bradford Cricket League have all benefitted from his sponsorship.

Jack Tordoff's own sporting preference is motor rallying, and he was a noted performer at rallies in his younger days. He also enjoys flying and owns his own plane and regularly flies from Leeds Bradford Airport on European business trips.

Jack first joined the Bradford City board in 1975 under the chairmanship of Bob Martin. City were a struggling Fourth Division side in those days, with crowds hovering not much above 3,000 or 4,000, and he played a leading part in giving them much needed financial support. He resigned in January 1978, along with fellow motor dealer Trevor Davidson, when they disagreed with the split-second decision to sack manager Bobby Kennedy, who had guided City to promotion to the Third Division the previous season. However, when the club went into receivership with £400,000 worth of debts five years later, he joined forces with former chairman Stafford Heginbotham to rescue City from oblivion.

They inherited Trevor Cherry as manager and Terry Yorath as coach, and two years later, with good management on and off the field, City gained promotion to the old Second Division as Third Division champions, ending a barren 48-year spell in the lower divisions.

However, triumph turned to tragedy when fire engulfed the old main stand at Valley Parade less than an hour after the Championship trophy had been paraded round the ground at the final match of the season, and 56 people lost their lives.

While the city was plunged into mourning, the football club had to carry on with business as best they could and found themselves tackling the demands of a higher division without a ground of their own. Eventually, they settled at the Odsal stadium, the home of Bradford Northern Rugby League club, but the pressure was overwhelming for them to move back to Valley Parade, and Jack Tordoff was put in charge of rebuilding the ground – a £2.6 million scheme. 'It was done in six months,' he recalled 'and we didn't pay a penny over budget.'

Tordoff succeeded Heginbotham as chairman in January 1988 and was criticised for not backing the then manager Terry Dolan in his quest for additional players to pursue City's promotion challenge. It's a criticism that Tordoff vigorously rebuts. City missed out on automatic promotion and were beaten by Middlesbrough in the Play-offs and then lost their two star players, Stuart McCall and John Hendrie, McCall to Everton for £850,000 and Hendrie to Newcastle for £500,000.

He provided Dolan with the proceeds of the sale of Hendrie and McCall to spend on new players. However, just over midway through the season, with the new look team only halfway up the table and out of both main Cup competitions, he sacked the manager and replaced him with Terry Yorath, who walked out on his job as Swansea manager to return to Valley Parade.

Unfortunately, Yorath's return was not a success, despite more money being spent on new players, and in January 1990 Jack Tordoff decided to sell his shares to a consortium led by Bradford travel agent David Simpson. City were in the middle of a bad run, and when things did not improve Simpson sacked Yorath, replaced him with John Docherty, and the club were relegated.

Tordoff admitted 'My interest was waning. I had taken Yorath from his job, and I could see me having to sack him. It just wasn't working the second time around. However, I left the club with assets of £1.5 million with no mortgage, a very small overdraft and owing hardly anything for players. All our monthly bills were paid on time, as was the VAT and National Insurance. I ran it as a business, not to be popular with the fans.'

Tordoff became life president after leaving the board and has continued to give generous support to the club through sponsorship and in other ways. For nine consecutive seasons, until the summer of 2006, he was City's shirt sponsor, and it is estimated he contributed £1.5 million in sponsorship during that period when cars for management and backroom staff are taken into account. He has also sponsored individual matches.

Bob Torrance

Date of birth: Unknown
Died: 24 April 1918

Bradford City record:
Appearances: League 161, FA Cup 18
Debut: 28 November 1908 v Everton

Also played for: Kirkintilloch Rob Roy

Scot Bob Torrance, a hero of City's FA Cup win, was one of was of several City players tragically killed during World War One.

Torrance joined the club from his home-town team Kirkintilloch Rob Roy and was nicknamed the Red Knight of Kirkintilloch because of the colour of his hair.

When Torrance arrived at the club in the 1907 close season he was an understudy to City's regular defenders. In fact, he didn't play a single match in his first season when City won the Second Division Championship.

However, he made his debut against Everton at the end of November the following season, and after that he gradually worked his way into the team, playing nine matches in that 1908-09 season – City's first in the top flight and eight the following campaign.

Torrance still wasn't a regular in that momentous 1910-11 season when City not only achieved their highest ever placing in Division One but won the FA Cup. He made 19 League appearances and two in the Cup, but was not in the side that drew 0-0 with Newcastle United in the Final at Crystal Palace.

However, manager Peter O'Rourke drafted him into the team as centre-half where he replaced the injured William Gildea, and he was one of the key players as City defied everything that Newcastle's highly-rated forward line could throw at them after captain Jimmy Speirs had given them a first-half lead.

The strong and competititve Torrance made 23 appearances the following season before establishing himself as first-choice centre-half over the next three seasons.

He missed only two League matches in 1912-13 and three matches the following campaign and also played 31 times in the League in 1914-15 before League football was suspended because of the war.

Torrance joined the Royal Field Artillery as a gunner and was killed on 24 April 1918 not far from Ypres in Belgium – just over six months before the war ended. His unit was supporting a West Riding Division near Poeringhe when it was hit by shelling and he lost an arm. He died a few days later when a field hospital where he was a patient was shelled.

Torrance has no known grave and is commemorated on the Tyne Cot Memorial to the Missing within sight of the grave of another City FA Cup-winning hero, captain Jimmy Speirs at Dochy Farm New British Cemetery near Ypres.

He made 161 League appearances spread over eight seasons, plus 18 in the FA Cup, but didn't score a single goal. He also played 52 wartime matches.

His last appearance was in a wartime regional match against Barnsley at Valley Parade in March 1917.

Whelan 'Polly' Ward

Date of birth: 15 June 1929

Bradford City record:
Appearances: League 149, FA Cup 7
Goals: League 37, FA Cup 5
Debut: 25 December 1948 v Oldham Athletic

Also played for: Ovenden, King's Lynn, Bradford Park Avenue, Nelson

The most striking feature of Whelan – known to everyone as Polly – Ward was his size – 5ft 2½in. Lack of height can be perceived as a handicap, but Ward still enjoyed a successful career at both ends of Bradford during the 1950s – a skilful inside-forward, who could score goals.

Born in the Ovenden district of Halifax, Ward had numerous setbacks before he fulfilled his desire to play League football. He had unsuccessful trials with Bradford Park Avenue, Leeds United, Hull City and Halifax Town before he made his mark with Bradford City. Ward also played local football for Ovenden before serving as an army despatch rider during World War Two.

City manager David Steele, who knew Ward from his spell at Huddersfield Town where he was on schoolboy forms, signed him as a 19-year-old amateur in November 1948, and after making his debut in a 2-1 win at Oldham on Christmas Day, he played regularly in the second half of the season and made 19 League appearances to the end of the campaign.

He became a full-time professional at the start of the following season but found himself in and out of the side as David Steele chopped and changed in his large squad.

His most successful season was in 1951-52, when he scored 12 goals in 34 matches, scoring in four successive matches towards the end of a season in which Steele resigned, and in the December he became the smallest centre-forward in the game when he played in that position against Lincoln City.

Otherwise he switched between inside-right and inside-left, and his sheer skilful play, low centre of gravity and his goalscoring opportunism around the six-yard area provided him with his fair share of goals.

Ward continued to play regularly for two seasons under new manager former Welsh international Ivor Powell, but he left City in August 1954 to join non-League King's Lynn.

However, he returned to League football in Bradford 12 months later to play for Park Avenue, and he played for four years in a good class Avenue team, scoring 31 goals in 108 League appearances.

He returned to non-League football in August 1959, by which time he was 30, joining Nelson, where he ended his playing career.

Dickie Watmough

Date of birth: 1912
Died: 1962

Bradford City record:
Appearances: League 94, FA Cup 4
Goals: League 25, FA Cup 1
Debut: 19 September 1931 v Bristol City

Also played for: Blackpool, Preston North End

Richard Watmough, known as Dickie, was one of the best local-born players to grace Valley Parade during the 1930s. Watmough came from Idle in the north of the city and appeared for local clubs Calverley, Thackley, Greengates United and Idle as a centre-forward before City signed him as an amateur in July 1931. He soon became a professional and established himself in City's Second Division team on the right wing, scoring goals in 34 League appearances in his first season.

However, after scoring 26 goals in 98 League and FA Cup he was transferred to Blackpool in October 1934, one of several outstanding players City sold in the 1930s to ease their financial problems.

Watmough was a success at Bloomfield Road, helping Blackpool to gain promotion to the First Division at the end of the 1936–37 season, and after playing 100 matches for them he was transferred to their local rivals Preston in November 1937 after Blackpool made it clear they wanted to sign their Scottish international centre-forward Frank O'Donnell. Preston insisted they would only sell O'Donnell if Watmough joined them in part exchange, and so, eventually, the Scottish international joined Blackpool, with Watmough and Jimmy McIntosh moving to Deepdale as Preston also received £8,000.

The move to Preston turned out to be a great success for Watmough for he collected an FA Cup-winners' medal after helping them to beat Huddersfield Town after extra-time in the Final at Wembley. Sadly, that was his last senior match as, after missing the 1938–39 season through injury, he retired during the war.

Watmough was also a talented cricketer and was once 12th man for Yorkshire.

Billy Watson

Date of birth: Unknown
Died: October 1950

Bradford City record:
Appearances: League 330, FA Cup 17
Goals: League 1
Debut: 27 August 1921 v Oldham Athletic

Also played for: Airdrieonians, Walsall

Billy Watson was one of many players that City signed from junior football in and around Glasgow in the first 20 years or so of their history. The wholehearted, hard tackling left-back was born at Larkhall and joined the Scottish League club Airdrieonians before signing for City in May 1921 for a club-record fee of £3,050. Watson made his debut in City's last season of First Division football and quickly made his mark, missing only three matches in that ill-fated campaign, and he went on to give City 10 years of excellent service, making 347 League and FA Cup appearances – 330 of them in the League.

City struggled after being relegated back to the Second Division and there followed five difficult seasons before they were relegated again – this time to the Third Division North, which had been formed when the Football League expanded after World War One – but Watson's consistency was one of the few highlights. He was appointed club captain in 1924-25 and missed only one match the following season.

Watson suffered the heartache of relegation for a second time with City when they finished bottom of the Second Division in 1927, but he had the satisfaction of helping them back to the Second Division when they won the Third Division North Championship two years later, missing only one match as partner to Northern Ireland international Sam Russell in what is regarded as one of the outstanding seasons in the club's long history.

He missed only four matches the following season – City's first campaign back in Division Two – but after playing in the first 10 matches of the next season he lost his left-back place to Sam Barkas as new manager Jack Peart began to re-shape his team. Peart signed Charlie Bicknell from Chesterfield to replace right-back Russell in the 1930 close season and shortly after that the famous Bicknell-Barkas full-back pairing began.

Watson scored only one goal for City and what a goal it was apparently. He was said to have scored from 10 yards inside his own half in a 2-1 home defeat against Portsmouth in October 1926.

He was also involved in an infamous off the field escapade that occurred during New Year celebrations in his first season at Valley Parade. The incident which has been passed down in City's folklore involved Watson and two fellow Scottish teammates, goalkeeper Jock Ewart and Tommy Robb. They were charged with being in enclosed premises not far from Valley Parade 'with intent to commit a felony', but, fortunately for the players, the Bradford magistrates believed their explanation that this was a 'ghost hunting' expedition – a foolish prank that went wrong.

The definitive version was explained by Watson himself, writing in the *Yorkshire Sports* some 26 years later. Writing about his days at City, he said 'The trouble started when three respectable Scottish citizens of Bradford were arrested by a platoon of policemen at the rear of a house at the bottom of Oak Avenue. The house was next to that of the Chief Constable of Bradford at that time, but the three Scots didn't know that and they must have disturbed him as they pushed his bedroom window up and started questioning him. They replied with a few harmless but accurate snowballs and told him to get back to bed after wishing him a Happy New Year.

'With the arrival of the police up went the window again. The arms – I mean the feet – of the law stood to attention so the three Scots then began to think there was something wrong. They knew it was when one of the bobbies whispered to one of the Scots who the All Highest really was and the police were told to arrest the "desperadoes". The three Scots were lodged in Manningham jail for the night, taken in a Black Maria in the morning to the Town Hall, put through all the routine there and then heard the case dismissed as "a foolish prank" on paying for damage to a house that had stood neglected for 20 years.

'The Scots were Jock Ewart, Tommy Robb and myself and that was the first and last mission of looking for ghosts. It started through a rumour that the house was supposed to be haunted. The house, by the way, was occupied a few months afterwards so the "desperadoes" must have done some good.'

Watson moved to Walsall in the Third Division North in August 1931 and played 35 matches in one season before retiring from the game and taking the Malt Shovel public house at Baildon. He died there in October 1950

Garry Watson

Date of birth: 7 October 1955

Bradford City record:
Appearances: League 263, FA Cup 10, League Cup 20
Goals: League 28, League Cup 2
Debut: 4 October 1972 v Chester

Also played for: Doncaster Rovers (loan), Halifax Town, Harrogate Town, Whitby Town
Managed: Farsley Celtic, Guiseley, Bridlington Town

Bradford City have had few more hard working and loyal players than Garry Watson, who enjoyed darting forward to have a shot at goal. The Bradford-born midfield player or full-back joined the club on schoolboy forms in November 1970, after being spotted by City centre-forward Norman Corner while he was coaching at Tong Comprehensive School.

Watson was still an apprentice when he made his League debut in the Fourth Division – a 1–0 home defeat against Chester as a 16-year-old in October 1972 – and he scored his first goal three days later on his 17th birthday in another defeat – this time 2–1 at Cambridge.

He became a full-time professional a year later when he was 18 and gradually established a regular place in 1975–76 – the season reached the FA Cup quarter-final, losing 1–0 at home to the eventual winners Southampton – although his FA Cup involvement was restricted to a substitute appearance in the 2–1 win at Shrewsbury in the third round.

Watson made 36 appearances, mainly in midfield, and scored seven goals the following season when City were promoted to Division Three under Bobby Kennedy and continued to be a regular for the next five seasons. He then suffered the heartache of relegation 12 months later and losing out on promotion on goal average in 1979–80 when he played mainly at left-back.

Of his 12 years at Valley Parade, Watson has no doubt that the Roy McFarland era that lasted a mere 18 months – from May 1981 to November 1982 – was the best. 'His man mangement skills were exceptional,' he recalls. 'He involved everyone. He was just finishing his career when he came to us, but I watched him play for England and he was arguably the best centre-half in the country. Unfortunately, he had trouble with his hamstring injuries and there were other good central defenders around at the time like Terry Butcher and Norman Hunter. When someone like Roy comes into the club you are keen to impress and you ask yourself what is he doing here.

'I always remember the first game he played in a training session – he flattened Bobby Campbell. When Bob got up Roy simply said "You train as you play. By that I mean fair, not over the top." It seemed to be a statement to everyone else that "I am not here for the ride." It was a privilege to play alongside him.'

Watson played 40 League matches, all at left-back, plus one as substitute, as City gained promotion under McFarland, finishing second to Sheffield United, but the match he recalls with most pleasure was a League Cup third-round tie at Ipswich, then managed by Bobby Robson, who had been voted European Team of the Year the season before. The team was full of big name players, George Burley, Mick Mills, Terry Butcher, Russell Osman, Paul Mariner, Alan Brazil and the Dutch pair Frans Thijssen and Arnold Muhren. Watson recalls scoring the goal that earned City a replay, which they lost 3–2 after extra-time, and being given the job of marking Thijssen.

After the promotion season, Watson's City career gradually wound down, and in October 1982 he went on loan to Doncaster Rovers, returning three months later. He made only nine appearances that season and at the end of the campaign he was put in charge of the reserves while still playing and scouting.

He made only four appearances in 1983–84 in what proved to be his final season at Valley Parade and left the club with a certain amount of ill feeling. Shortly after he was awarded a testimonial after completing 10 years' service, the club went into receivership which badly hampered his plans. 'The testimonial never really happened because of the receivership and I left with £1,200 severance pay and only £1,100 from the testimonial fund,' he said. Watson also says the club promised him a testimonial match, but went back on their word. He had a game against Derby County's Championship-winning side lined up through Roy McFarland, but it never happened.

Halifax Town gave him the chance to revive his League career when he joined them as a part-time professional in July 1984, teaming up with Ces Podd, who had been released by City that summer, and made 21 more appearances at the Shay that took his career tally to 338 in League and Cup – 299 and 31 goals for City, including 263 appearances and 28 goals in the League.

After his League career was over, Watson enjoyed a variety of non-League experiences – two years with Whitby Town where former Leeds United goalkeeper David Harvey was player-manager, two years as manager of Farsley Celtic, assistant manager and then manager at Guiseley and manager at Bridlington Town before a spell as a scout with Scarborough.

Since then Watson has forged a successful career as a carpet fitter with a shop in the Eccleshill district of Bradford.

Bobby Webb

Date of birth: 29 November 1933

Bradford City record:
Appearances: League 208, FA Cup 23, League Cup 2
Goals: League 59, FA Cup 4, League Cup 4
Debut: 20 August 1955 v Oldham Athletic

Also played for: Leeds United, Walsall, Torquay United

Peter Jackson made some shrewd signings during his six-year spell as Bradford City manager, but none better than Bobby Webb. The Altofts miner was a manager's dream – a goalscoring winger, whose consistency was a byword among teammates and supporters alike. He also played at inside-forward, but it was as an orthodox outside-right who liked to cut in and shoot that most City supporters will remember him.

Webb was born in the heart of the Yorkshire coalfield in the mining village of Altofts, and after gaining local representative honours Leeds United signed him as a 15-year-old, but he had to do two years' National Service before he made his debut for their reserve team that played in the Central League. He also played for United Northern Intermediate League team that won the League Cup between 1950 and 1952.

However, he found difficulty breaking into United's first team. He made his debut against Brentford in March 1954 alongside the great John Charles but had made only three first-team appearances when Leeds gave him a free transfer in March 1955, and he joined Walsall. After only four months at Walsall, he returned to West Yorkshire to become one of Jackson's signings in his first close season at Valley Parade.

Webb, who was a part-time footballer while working as a miner, was an instant success with City and was leading scorer with 18 goals in 40 League appearances in his first season as City recovered from narrowly avoiding having to seek re-election the season before by finishing a respectable eighth. Interestingly, his wing partner, outside-left Johnny Simm, who joined City from Bury four months before Webb, was second leading scorer with 14 goals, having played in all 46 League matches.

Webb didn't score as many goals the following season but still managed 11 as he missed only two League matches, but he suffered from injury in 1957-58, managing only 19 matches, scoring three goals as City finished third and earned their place in the national Third Division following the scrapping of the regional sections.

However, he was back on the goals trail the following season, scoring 12 in 38 matches, but missed the last seven matches when City finished 11th in the Third Division.

The 1959-60 season will always be remembered for a magnificent FA Cup run that saw them reach the fifth round before being beaten 5-0 in a replay away to future League champions Burnley. Webb played in all eight Cup games – three of the five ties went to replays – and scored in the thrilling 2-2 draw against Burnley in the Valley Parade mud as City lost a 2-0 lead and were forced to go to Turf Moor for a replay. Webb also scored nine in 40 League matches and was used as a makeshift centre-forward in five matches near the end of the season in place of the injured Derek Stokes.

Webb played only 19 League matches, scoring seven goals, as City were relegated, but had the distinction of scoring one of the goals that enabled City to beat Manchester United at home 2-1 in the first season of the League Cup – a match played in front of only 4,670 spectators on a midweek afternoon in November because there were no floodlights at Valley Parade at that time.

Webb managed only 11 League appearances the following season – City's first in the Fourth Division – but scored a hat-trick in their 4-3 home defeat against Aston Villa in the League Cup and played at Arsenal in the FA Cup third round when they lost 3-0.

He was transferred to Torquay in the summer of 1962, having scored 59 goals in 208 League matches in seven seasons at Valley Parade and eight goals in 25 Cup games. He played a further 49 League matches and scored 12 goals in two seasons at Torquay before he was forced to retire at 29 after breaking his leg.

David Wetherall

Date of birth: 14 March 1971

Bradford City record:
Appearances: League 258, FA Cup 9, League Cup 10
Goals: League 16, FA Cup 1, League Cup 2
Debut: 7 August 1999 v Middlesbrough

Also played for: Sheffield Wednesday, Leeds United
Managed: Bradford City (caretaker player-manager)

When Bradford City gained promotion to the Premiership in May 1990, manager Paul Jewell decided they needed a new central-defender with experience of top-flight football. So, he signed David Wetherall from Leeds United for a club record £1.4 million, and what a terrific capture he has proved to be.

However, whatever else he achieves at Valley Parade, nothing will surpass the crucial goal he scored against Liverpool 12 minutes into the final match of City's first season in the Premiership. The issue was simple – City needed to win to have a chance of staying up, Liverpool also needed to win to ensure Champions League football at Anfield. Who among City supporters could have imagined what drama would unfold on that Sunday afternoon in May 2000? For, Wetherall headed the goal that ensured that City survived against all the odds and proved the pundits wrong.

It crowned a fine first season at Valley Parade for Wetherall as he played in every one of City's 38 Premiership matches, and he said 'I know people focus on that goal, but there were some significant matches in the build up to that game. We went to Sunderland, who had an impressive home record and were high in the League. No one gave us a chance, but John Dreyer scored the only goal of the game. That win closed the gap on the teams above us and gave us a light at the end of the tunnel and a belief that we could do it.'

When Wetherall joined City after making more than 200 League and Cup appearances for Leeds, little could he have realised what a roller-coaster life he would experience – a dramatic Premiership survival, three relegations, two administrations, a career threatening injury and a three-month spell as caretaker player-manager in 2006–07 that ended with City dropping into the fourth tier of English football.

He said 'Team spirit and hard work pulled us through our first season in the Premiership, and we won a good few games that we had no right to win like our first match at Middlesbrough, where we managed to keep things tight and then nick a late goal. Lack of expectation in the Liverpool match took a lot of pressure off us and allowed us to go out and play.'

A month after the Liverpool match, there was drama of a different kind when Paul Jewell resigned to go to Sheffield Wednesday. Wetherall recalls 'I was on holiday when I had a message on the answer phone. I was shocked and amazed. That was a huge blow for us, and I have no doubt that if Paul Jewell had stayed he would have signed a different type of player that summer. Who knows, but I think things would have been totally different.'

Wetherall admits that doubts about City's survival in their second Premiership season started when they failed to pick up points in the early part of the campaign, but soon he was having problems of his own. 'I had been struggling with a groin injury since the end of the previous season, and it just gave way in a match at Derby,' he said. 'Ultimately, I had two operations on the groin and another operation to cure a related problem. At one stage I thought I might be hanging up my boots, but fortunately I managed to get the problems sorted.' Injuries affected Wetherall for the next two seasons, but he eventually regained his fitness and has not only been a regular for the last four seasons, but an inspirational captain and a commanding defender.

He was appointed captain after Stuart McCall left to join Sheffield United in May 2002, and soon he was involved in delicate negotiations regarding contracts after the club went into administration. He said 'The problems came to the surface when it became clear that we were not going to go straight back up into the Premiership. It was well documented that Benny Carbone, Dan Petrescu and David Hopkin were on top Premiership money. For a club that were not in the Premiership, that was ruinous – the club simply could not sustain it.'

Wetherall was given the opportunity to do some coaching after Colin Todd succeeded Bryan Robson during the 2004 administration and the subsequent relegation, and he was placed in temporary charge when City sacked Todd in February 2007, but he could not prevent City from being relegated. At the end of the season, the club appointed McCall as manager and he re-appointed Wetherall as captain for the new campaign.

Jock Whyte

Date of birth: 7 May 1921
Died: 1998

Bradford City record:
Appearances: League 236, FA Cup 15
Goals: League 2
Debut: 2 September 1950 v Hartlepool United

Also played for: Bedloy Juniors, Forth Rangers, Falkirk, Wigan Athletic

Scot Jock Whyte joined City in the 1950 close season and was a regular right-back in his seven seasons at Valley Parade, making 251 League and FA Cup appearances, many of them as partner to George Mulholland. In fact, the first names on the team sheet in the mid-1950s were usually Smith, Whyte, Mulholland. Those names had a distinctive ring about them for supporters of an older generation.

Whyte joined his first club in Lanarkshire, Bedloy Juniors, after finishing his studies. From there he had a spell with Forth Rangers before he joined Falkirk during the 1944–45 season and played there for five years before moving to Bradford City in August 1950 at the age of 29 as manager David Steele tried to re-shape his side after City had narrowly missed having to apply for re-election for the second season in a row.

For the next six seasons Whyte was a regular in the side, missing only four matches in his first season, three matches in 1952–53, one match in 1953–55 and four in 1955–56. In modern football, full backs are all purpose players, often playing the ball out of defence to build up a flowing move or running on the overlap to join the attack and being able to cross the ball like the traditional wingers used to do. Jock did none of these things. He was a no frills, no nonsense out-and-out defender whose job was to mark, tackle and generally frustrate his winger and then clear the ball upfield.

The only blot on his Valley Parade career came on Boxing Day 1955 when he was sent for a bad foul. To see a player sent off is a fairly common occurrence in these days of red and yellow cards, but in the mid-1950s it was a rare event, and when Whyte received his marching orders that was the first time a City player had been sent off since another right-back, John Smith, was dismissed against Chesterfield on Easter Monday, March 1937.

Whyte lost his regular place in the 1956–57 season, being replaced for much of the campaign by fellow Scot Malcolm Currie, who joined City in the 1956 close season. Jock made only six appearances in his final season so it was no surprise when he was released in the 1957 close season having chalked up an impressive 236 League matches, scoring two goals and 15 FA Cup games.

Whyte joined Wigan Athletic, then a non-League club, but played for only one more season before retiring from football. In retirement, Jock spent several years scouting for Sheffield United, looking for junior players.

A proud Scotsman, Jock took a great interest in his first League club Falkirk. They provided the opposition for his testimonial match in 1955 – in those days players were normally granted a benefit after five years' service – and, after he died in 1998 his ashes were scattered on Falkirk's ground.

George Williamson

Date of birth: 13 September 1925
Died: 1994

Bradford City record:
Appearances: League 223, FA Cup 12
Goals: League 31, FA Cup 2
Debut: 14 October 1950 v Rotherham United

Also played for: Middlesbrough, Chester City, Colwyn Bay, Oswestry Town
Managed: Colwyn Bay

The versatile George Williamson was born at Newcastle and played for Newcastle Boys before he joined Middlesbrough. Unfortunately, he could not break into Newcastle's first team, and after two years playing in their reserve sides he decided to join Chester in the Third Division North in 1947. That move gave him the chance of regular first-team football and he made 75 League appearances in three seasons at Chester before he joined City in the 1950 close season – one of an influx of new players as manager David Steele recast his team following two disappointing seasons in which the club were forced to apply for re-election and only just missed suffering the same humiliation the following season.

A tall player, Williamson scored nine goals in 18 appearances in his first season as he fought to establish himself at Valley Parade, but eventually he became an indispensable member of the team with his ability to play in a variety of positions – centre-half, right-half, left-half, inside-forward – an undoubted asset.

His last three seasons at Valley Parade proved to be his best. He missed only two League matches in 1954–55, when he was also leading scorer – albeit with a modest six goals – as City narrowly missed having to seek re-election once again and prospered under new manager Peter Jackson. He was also one of five ever presents the following season – the first full campaign of Jackson's managerial era – and missed only five games in what proved to be his final season.

After seven years' service, Williamson was awarded a benefit and City beat Scottish League Airdrieonians in his benefit match at Valley Parade in April 1957. He left the club that summer having made 235 League and FA Cup appearances, scoring 33 goals, to join non-League North Wales club Colwyn Bay, and he later became their player manager. He ended his career with Oswestry Town in 1960 but continued his involvement with football as a local referee in the Wirrall and as secretary of the Ellesmere Port Sunday League.

I got to know him when we formed the Bradford City and Park Avenue Ex-Players' Association. He was still in love with the game more than 20 years after his retirement and continued his connection with football, not only by serving local footballers as a referee and administrator in his own district, but by regularly making a round trip of some 160 miles to renew acquaintances with his old teammates in the ex-players' association.

Dean Windass

Date of birth: 1 April 1969

Bradford City record:
Appearances: League 216, FA Cup 11, League Cup 12
Goals: League 76, FA Cup 3, League Cup 6
Debut: 9 March 1999 v Sunderland

Also played for: Hull City (twice, once on loan), Aberdeen, Oxford United, Middlesbrough, Sheffield Wednesday (loan), Sheffield United

With 239 League and Cup appearances and 85 goals to his name, Dean Windass has a honoured place in Bradford City's history. However, the 38-year-old striker – loved by his own fans, not so popular with opposing supporters – left the club in January 2007 to join Hull City, first on loan and then in a permanent deal.

Chairman Julian Rhodes sprang a surprise when he allowed leading scorer Windass to leave City, but the club needed the money to pay urgent bills, and by letting him go they not only saved on his wages but received a six-figure loan fee. So, while City badly missed the goals Windass would surely have supplied and were subsequently relegated, the striker scored eight goals during his loan spell to keep Hull in the Championship and during the summer the Humberside club completed a deal that could rise to £250,000 depending on appearances.

Windass, with two years to run on his contract, said 'To go back to my home town is special – I would never have left Bradford City for anybody else. Of course, I was happy to go to Hull, but I also did it to help the club. Julian Rhodes wanted to pay the wages for January and February and the loan was a way of doing that, but seeing Bradford get relegated was a massive disappointment. If Bradford had stayed in League One I would have stayed, but I felt I had a lot more to offer than League Two. I have never been a big-headed person, but my job was to go out and score goals for Bradford City and my record was very good. It was just a pity that we couldn't get back to the Championship where the club belongs'.

Windass's connection with City began in March 1999 when he joined the club from Oxford United in a £950,000 deal. Manager Paul Jewell wanted to strengthen his squad to make sure of promotion to the Premiership, and when City duly gained promotion at the end of the season the fee rose to £1 million, which made Windass City's third £1 million player in less than 12 months, Lee Mills and Isaiah Rankin were the others.

The following season was Windass's first in the Premiership, and he was determined to make it a success. He recalls 'I did not go on holiday that summer because I wanted to be in perfect shape for the Premiership. I trained every day that summer and it was worth it because the season went well – I scored 10 goals from midfield and Bradford stayed up. Pundits said we would be relegated, but we proved them wrong'.

Paul Jewell left in the summer after disagreements with chairman Geoffrey Richmond and, with City facing relegation the following March, Windass left for Middlesbrough in a £600,000 deal. He recalls: 'Bradford City were struggling at the time at the bottom of the League, and Geoffrey Richmond told me the club were going to offer me a new contract, but if they were relegated "it won't be the contract you want" so I moved to Middlesbrough and playing for them was the highlight of my career'.

Windass moved on a free transfer to Sheffield United in November 2002 after an approach from his former City teammate Stuart McCall, who, by then, was player-coach at Bramall Lane. He helped them to reach the Play-off Final and played in the semi-finals when they beat Nottingham Forest over two legs, but 'fell out' with manager Neil Warnock and watched Wolves beat them 3-0 in the Final in a pub. 'I had the option of a new contract, but I had to tell Neil Warnock I couldn't play for him again, and when I had a phone call from then chairman Gordon Gibb I signed for Bradford under Nicky Law'.

City had survived one administration crisis the previous summer, and the following year their future was placed in doubt with another spell in administration during which they were relegated to League One, the third tier of English football, after Bryan Robson had succeeded Nicky Law. Colin Todd, who had been Robson's number two, succeeded him as manager in the summer of 2004, and the following season Windass scored 28 goals and 20 more goals the following season, although City had to settle for a mid-table place in both campaigns. He was so successful at Valley Parade that he was top scorer for four seasons after returning to City from Bramall Lane and is third in the club's all-time scoring list behind Bobby Campbell and Frank O'Rourke.

Although Windass has enjoyed a successful career, he struggled to break into League football after being released by his home-town club as a teenager. He recalls 'I was lucky enough to get another chance at Hull when I was 21 thanks to Terry Dolan when I was playing North Ferriby. I owe everything to Terry Dolan. All I wanted was a chance, and he gave me that at Hull. On the day I signed, I vowed to myself I would never go back to working on a building site at £140 per week. I really did think my chance had gone because after leaving Hull I had trials at Sunderland, Cambridge and York, but none of them worked out'.

Windass scored 57 goals in 176 appearances in four years at Hull, then moved to Aberdeen in a £700,000 deal. He spent almost three years at Pittodrie scoring 34 goals in 95 appearances before joining Oxford United for £425,000. He had a great goalscoring record at Oxford with 18 in 38 matches, but nine months later he was on the move again – this time for his first spell at Valley Parade.

BV - #0024 - 260226 - C0 - 234/156/11 - PB - 9781780914466 - Gloss Lamination